Fresh Air and The Story of Molecule

JOHN GALLAS was born in 1950 in Wellington, New Zealand. He came to England in 1971 to study Old Icelandic at Oxford, and stayed. He has worked for many years as a teacher with the Leicestershire Behaviour Support Team. He has published seven collections of poetry with Carcanet Press and edited the anthology of world poetry *The Song Atlas* (2002). Swims like a fish, cycles like a windmill.

D1353618

JOHN GALLAS

Fresh Air and *The Story of Molecule*

CARCANET

First published in Great Britain in 2012 by

Carcanet Press Limited
Alliance House
Cross Street
Manchester M2 7AQ

www.carcanet.co.uk

A CIP catalogue record for this book is available from the British Library

ISBN 978 1 84777 097 4

The publisher acknowledges financial assistance from Arts Council England

Typeset by XL Publishing Services, Tiverton
Printed and bound in England by SRP Ltd, Exeter

Contents

FRESH AIR

Fresh Air

Four Thoughts from Abroad

1 blue sky in Porvoo...

Blue sky in Porvoo, the cloud pulled thin,
nearly-torn white, and grey for its shapes,

flat, low and yellow behind the church roof,
treaclewood tiles bright with snow,

then blue sky...
Why is it always behind everything,

that drapeless blue?:
that cross, that far, covered hill.

2 deconstructing the Turkish flag over Diyarbakir

A hot heaven, one star and a crescent moon
above Diyarbakir, hung in dark green.

The star fires beside
the moon's dark-yellow back.

When the sky turns red, and the star
sails into the turned moon's curve,

You Are Lucky To Be A Turk.

3 execution of a Chinese con man

Man Ling sold drugs
made out of baking ingredients.

People believed him and died.
He was shot by the sea in Baozhong.

He chose a sailor's suit to die in.
Which shows a kind of care.

4 *scene seen from a plane over South Asia*

Tiny golden detail.
The plane beats over Belangkor
against the sun's falling face.

Lagoons and inlets, syrup-twists in rivers,
liquid land and light-loop flicks.
Here and there, drops of lacquered milk.

Ah, it seems the answer to a dream.
Who argue over traffic too,
and fight for lovers.

A poem from Home and Russia, Number 1

Sputnik over En Zed

The rugby field's on fire. Its giant Sheriffs,
H and H, stand guard between the darkness
and my dreams. The grownups smoke while we,
whose lives have hardly started, turn and burn
our sausages on green and whittled sticks.

Sparks shanghai the stars. Our mothers' fear,
discovered in the shiver of their hats,
provokes my cowboy confidence that I,
redhot and wild, keep up this Sausage Sizzle
and the World, ten-gallonned on my head –

whose fatness leaves no room for doubt. But they,
who feel they think they know with age some end
to all this food and fire and light, look up
without the make-believe of hope, and watch
while Something bleeps and blinks through Outer Space.

I've ditched my star. The Sputnik jitter runs
in circles round me still, and my corral
is not OK: and somewhere out there, somewhere
out of range it winds its question marks
across the sky, and bleeps at childish law.

The goalposts gleam. We wrap our sausages
in bread and butter. Mother smiles. It's gone.
My fingers smear and shine. I spin my Colt:
blam-blam! The smoke half-clears. Our red position
glitters and is gone. We drive back home.

Five P.each Pomes

1   the price of goats' milk

The price of goats' milk
has never gone down
in my lifetime.
But there is still hope.

2   gecrong

Byrhtnoth fell.
Splang!
And one by one
his Big Protectors
too.
Crish! Crosh! Crash!
We struggle to stand.
Death is a decline
to the horizontal.

3   flowers

Everybody likes flowers,
even though they were not made for Us.

4   do not

Do not clean
the inside of
a car without
an Elf attachment.

5 *I fink*

I have a feeling
that Fen End
is finking.

Two Still Lifes Painted at the Subject

1 Ode to Autumn

for Sarah

A throttled bramble, raspberry horror, jerks
in coldbright wind: and rearing, throe-mad, scores
the weak white sky with thorns. Autumn works
its pogrom: frost-limp nettles, gasping haws,
the red and yellow fit of strangled fruit,
and traitored colours of the fire become
the symptoms of complaint. A bandaged sun
drills glassglare puddles in the rut-mud, numb
and white. And every prickle, stock and root
shakes and shuts. Unknown black birds hoot
the memory of plenty: there is none.

Dull evergreens, expressionless and cold:
bonestraw grassclumps: clouds laid on the sky
like ointment gauze: whipped withies hold
their last giant bowl-leaves hazard-high.
Who has not seen you, stretchered on the wind,
amidst your battlefield? Two silos freeze
faroff in cold-singed fields: and cows present
their frozen rumps, unmoving, to the trees.
The scratching fitful hedgerows, wrack and ruined,
hem the lane: and branchfalls, sodden-skinned,
rimed and rotten, finger where you went.

Who saw you pass this monstrous oak, and take
its crown, with all the cruelty of spring?
It stands here, yellow-palsied, with the ache
of nuded greatness, sadly whispering
its summer roar. Its mighty arms drop yellow
favours on the amputated mush
below: and suddenly, the world teems
with falling splendour, and a falling hush.
The brambles still. The sun lies white and low.
And on one branch, its last leaf gone, a crow
spreads its baffled, wind-nipped wings, and screams.

2 *banana*

This is the new poetry. I'll draw
a banana: without one simile,
one onomatopoeia, metaphor,
syllepsis, assonance, cacophony,
oxymoronising,
asyndetonising –
nothing. Just the thing.

Where the poet's brain
is absent, and the plain
truth may entertain.

This banana is yellow; marked with blue,
brown and black in-pressions here and there;
its thin skin-segment lines curved and skew
along its length; the stalk's fibrous tear
flattened shrivelledly.
It is a little shiny.

That is poetry,
which is not me.

Three Site-Specific Poems

1   poem to be read by the fire

we are a little older
since the last time
we laid and lit this fire

consider then
how best to use
our greater experience

in matters of love
and time
amidst the laws of gravity

2   poem to be read at a swimming lesson

breathing here
will be taught
as a skill

thus tomorrow and forever
we will be conscious
of our involuntary airings
of every automatic in and out

which may have
tragic or fatal
psychosomatic
consequences
and lead to madness

3   *poem to be read while cycling*

Ah the wind in your ribbons
isn't it grand

like a soul borne on a body
like a polished knight ahorse
a floating fire in a funnel

a small convulsion in one knee
a slight agony
where the pedal and the heel
misalign

isn't it grand
how we fly
how we fly

Three Poems Written in Mongolia

1   the Mongolian Women's Orchestra

enter the Mongolian Women's Band
with
the years,

whose music, theirs and theirs, like language learned,
inevitable, red and super-sound,
outplays the days the days that made it mine

and beauty beauty adds to it — its stir,
its wink, its melt, and anything that shines —
this is *The Horse that Overtook the Wind:*

the little men that ride the plain
on hearts that will not race again
whose hoofbeats knock on heaven's door —
they will not come back anymore

the history of hope is short:
it has one chapter — Youth. I thought
that memories would make me wise
but nothing comes as no surprise

across the windy open spaces
briefly bright their shining faces
do with beauty then are gone —
the horses gallop on and on

and if I played my darndest darndest card,
who have no beauty now, no more, what tricks
I take have not the hearts they had before.

The Horse that Overtook the Wind is done,
and beauty beauty raced it well — its stir,
its wink, its melt, and anything that shines

exit the Mongolian Women's Band
with
the years

2 *bits of Karakorum*

fine brown rain falls
out of complicated clouds
on a shiny green tarpaulin
unevenly on the ground

where our plastic plates
blue and pink overflow
their sour vegetables
quietly in a square

singly and in pairs
we are somewhere
out amongst the acres
of ever-
lastingness
picking up bits

our red and yellow parkas
flare not like flames
but chemically
wet and distant
from age
and each other

the rain rustles round my hood
out of the muddying dust I pick
a brimstone clog of burned brick
I am standing where it stood

and I will fall in rotless red
someone waves like semaphore
I don't know what the world is for
clouds blossom overhead

someone else's boot
has pushed its print
briefly into
the earth interrupted
with half-
cracked cinders

bits of the city fall
slowly to the ground
when I look up
and turn back
to the van
too slowly to see

bits of pickled cabbage
inch over the plastic edges
of our plates and splash
slowly on the green tarpaulin

clouds rear like empires
above us and quietly
singly and in pairs
we burn the air red and yellow

3   man in a yellow del

What was yellow before I saw this?
And what, Man? Maybe some egg, some sun,
some Hollywoodwork – some half-hack apprentice
thing, before the masterpiece was done:
the looking-end, the start of memory:
and I could hang on both infinitely
as long as they go now away from me.

This del hung on its dummy would not look
so well: nor yet this man in blue; but yet,
like alcohol and acid mixed and shook
to singularity, they breathe the blet
of estern apples on a poet-tree:
and I could hang on that infinitely
as long as it goes now away from me.

And when the best is done before the end,
what is there left but thinking of it? Some
die of this; while other co-extend
the quick-scent of their souls and make a sum
of disparates, and court inconstancy:
and I could hang on this infinitely
as long as it goes now away from me.

Introduction and Exercise Concerning the Kenning,
After Snorri Sturluson's 'Skáldskaparmál'

1 introduction to the kenning

Let us imagine first people have things called Heads.
Well of course they do.
A Head should be referred to as
Spine-Shipment, Neck-Cargo,
Hatworld, Brain-Land, Cap-Couch,
Hairgarden, Eyebrow-Supporter,
Scalpstretcher, Ear-Mug,
Eye-Pudding or Mouth-Preserver.

The Mouth should be referred to as
Tongue-Cabin, Tooth-Villa,
Word-Ranch, Gums-Flat
or, maybe, Lip-Bungalow.

Teeth should be referred to as
Gob-Rocks, Word-Buddies,
Tongue-Tombstones. And the Tongue
should be referred to as
Mouth-Gun.

2 a simple kenning exercise

Let us take th'unvarnished line

Billyboy got shot in the head

Now, a Billy may be referred to as
Gruff, Giddy, Getting-On-My,
Squint-Features, Horn-Rammikin,
or Buckarooniedoodle.

A Squint may be called
Eye-Squeezy, and the Eyes
may be called Phizzog-Moons.
Thus, so far, Billy is a Phizzog-Moons-Squeezy-Looker.

To continue, the Phizzog (or Face)
may be referred to as
Neck-Balloon, and Moons as
Night-Sailors. Thus, Billy
may be referred to as
★ *Neck-Balloon-Night-Sailor-Squeezy-Looker*

Let us consider Boy. A Small Man.
Who should be referred to as
Little Bar-Leaning Pardner.
Now Bar may be a Drinking-Hedge
and Hedge a Field-Muff
and Drinking a Mouth-Tide
and Mouth a Tooth-Villa:
thus Boy should be referred to as
★ *Small Tooth-Villa-Tide-Field-Muff Angled Pardner*

To get shot is to be Bullet-Buggered,
Eat Lead, Swallow da Dumdum,
Suck-a-Slug or be a Wadmagnet.
Now a Slug may be a Birdie of Death
and a Birdie a Moon-Cruiser
and the Moon a Night-Opticle
and Death a Mind-Remover
and the Mind a Brain-Book:
thus Was Shot should be referred to as
★ *sucked a Night-Opticle-Cruiser of Brain-Book-Remover*

And lastly, Head. Which may be referred to as
Hairgarden, as we have seen above.
Now Hair may be Skull-Plantation
or Thoughtthicket or Scalp-Crop
and a Garden may be
Veg-Bearer, Mother of Gobbles,
Seedsucker or Potato-Shroud.

Thus, Head should be referred to as
* *Brain-Thicket Potato-Shroud*

Thus, th'unvarnished line

Billyboy got shot in the head

becomes the beautiful

Neck-Balloon-Night-Sailor-Squeezy-Looker Small Tooth-Villa-Tide-Field-Muff Angled Pardner sucked a Night-Opticle-Cruiser of Brain-Book-Remover in the Thought-Thicket Potato-Shroud

A Text with txt

MOT for Prisoner MH 8313

B-*ump,* down goes the seat.	I
I lie in the car in a layby oh some-	
where amazed. *The car passed.*	m
The steeringwheel is plastic-hot.	
Clouds bubble along the wingmirror	rIting
like TV, like sun, like everything.	
I doze delighted. Split light sticks	2 tell
lemon splinters in your seat. The brake	
on bronze. I miss you more each awful second.	u
Your seat hangs its headrest, blazing blue,	
loose, a little, this sadness, and we	the
changed gear here ...	
somewhere ...	cR

zzz ... the top branches of a tree	pRst
still screwed up in the wind;	
a few leaves	its
ripped upwards still	
into a mustardgas sky	MOT
where birds are thrown still	
and swoop blown; ah,	Bcoz
it's a picture ...	
let me out, let me	it
back to my time ...	
finish this sentence ... zzz	cRnt

Jed lifts your bonnet.	w8
Light–goldfish burst out, swimming. In this	
brilliant sea he sees each oiled piece,	2 hold
fluid brake, working works,	
and wants you back ...	u

... and we wait, we three, passed,
in this layby oh some-
where amazed, to hold you
like sun, like TV, like everything,
in flakes of lemon light: impatient,
whole and slow, cut down with smiles
and start our lying-watch again.

&

Bwicht

the

mechanic

Five Excuses

1 *homework*

I did not do my homework
because
the meadow was full of umbels.

2 *wedding*

I cannot come to your wedding
because
there is a blindworm in the wainscot.

3 *listening*

I wasn't listening
because
the blossom is looking cereous.

4 *football*

We lost this afternoon
because
the fog is shapen like a trumpet.

5 *writing*

I did not write anything today
because
I was worried about Saskatoon.

Poem Written After a Dream Dreamed at the Exact Time of the Death of Luciano Pavarotti

the Apotheosis of Pavarotti

and extra angels for the weight of it
nose-dove, sleepy eyes and yawnthump wings,
alarmed at five o'clock and a jumborous soul
all bubbled out and breathless to collect
from Modena, the air all water-white,

out of a still, dough bed,
easy pulled and plain as buttered light,
all lightness couched through a red roof, up
th'undarkling treetops, dampbirds, brume,
and all dark-shoulder morning things,

unwinding sheets fall wet and white,
curl, leave, drop, flutter,
down to the darkdew grass, the hairy,
heavy beast and soul, which after all are one,
that wakes again as saved souls do,

all hanging in their extra arms,
you have forgot my handkerchief,
and the hanky angel nose-dove too,
thuddering through thick unsunny clouds,
the big, unwound pyjamas flutter, curl, drop, leave,

and the bunch shoot off suddenly at the sun,
whoosh! and the angel at his hairy ear
whispers *Sing, Luciano — eternity can hear!*
he lifts the cold delivered hanky high
and barrel-naked bellows every corner bright.

Poems Describing my Four Favourite Pictures in the National Gallery

1

A man pranceth forth
with a large pot
and a tree.

A young man embraceth
a haystook and looketh about
moideredly.

A fat man holdeth up
a gleamy glass
beyond his buttons.

A old man warmeth his hands
at a little box,
much garnitured for the cold.

2

A man in a hat
casts his legs
clatter at a
wee bright flame.
Haste and horror demand
his hand before his mouth.

3

A soldier is dead.
Largely.
By his death are a bubble
and a smoke-squig.
All fugacious.

4

O'er silver'd water
a boat does not go
but has been to
and fro on the bright concurrent
under a well-mannered sky.

Two Poems Written in Scotch Drizzle

1 in the graveyard at Campbeltown with a wet beanie

Sub-Lieutenant H. Mackay
left his home in Atawhai
and died beneath a German bomb
that did not care where he was from.

And he has swapped his bellbirds for the rain,
and won't go home again.

Peter Alexander Lound
went the other way around
and got the flu in Ngawhatu
as many gold prospectors do.

And he has changed his kirk for kōkōtea,
and cannot come back here.

2 the statues of Glasgow and Campbeltown

Burns, Watt,
Peel and Scott
take the air
in George Square.

Far away, in Campbeltown,
Mackinnon looks obscurely down
upon the bus-stop and the grass:

triumphs of our Dust in Brass:

cast and tall,
who weather all:
storm, birds,
darkness, words ...

So let you stand, unknown and cold,
against the rain, and not grow old;
iron to my faithless Will –

forgotten, but immortal still.

Two Norfolk Beach Poems

1   *sunrise at Brancaster Beach*

Bent with gentle heaviness, the old,
bald head of earth, explained in yellow light,
gets licked to life again. The sea looks white,
like bitten skin; the wrinkled sand feels cold.
This is the end of night: and from its sleep,
whose sweet corruption burns me like a match
just struck, the world is laboured out. A patch
of orange cloud turns pale. I shiver. Deep,
deep beyond the air where words, ideas
and minds are kept convinced, I only see
the churning of great planets – one with me,
the rest without. I yawn. The sun appears
and all the earth is warm. And even I
applaud with half a smile the bloodless sky.

2   *the Golden Sands Amusements, Hunstanton, on St Lucy's Day*

The shortest day's longest night: fog
and freeze. I walk the coldbed caravans
behind the bitter floodwall. Chilly cans
crumple and oo, tin-mouthed. Somewhere a dog
hacks. Ice, mud, shit.
Shut-up, starveling, soul-bit,
I keep my heart in.

My ears glint rime like stars. Fog and freeze
jitter on the sea's frost-froth. Blank
weight, black sky, presses dank
raw ink through everything. I gulp. I sneeze.
I tiptoe over grass.
It growls like crackled glass.
My goosey skin.

Suddenly, from a night-ript gash,
this yellow shockthing yells into my eyes:
all-electric birdie, cackling, house-size,
chinglechingle flickerfun and flash,
its glassmouth open wide,
nothing but yellow inside
and a brass din.

The last great Frolic Cash-Bird: left behind
when all the chatt'ring others flapped away
to winter in Las Vegas. Damned to stay
in fog and freeze, nipt and golden-blind,
the Warbler jigs alone
on ice. I am chill to the bone
and my heart within.

A plastic policeman winks me in: a clown
beeps: and every yellow short-circuit madness
hops and signals. I am pierced with sadness.
This frantic, empty thing. I clitter down
the dark halfroad-halfpark.
The earth is cold and dark,
and my heart within.

I like electric days. Like anyone.
And birdy-bulbs will do till summerlight.
You've got my heart. Maybe I wasn't right
to be alone today. This isn't fun.
Ah, when love is gone,
then I'll be cold John
and let it in.

Three Translations of Nineteenth-Century Folk-Songs

1   from Rolovia

Springle, Springle,
Come gather 'pon the tabard,
Ah green grow the gooseberries,
My darling has gone to sea,
Springle, Springle,
And the extemporaneous rose.

Springle, Springle,
Come hornpipe on my heart,
Ah his ghost is green and gory,
My wimple cost me a purse,
Springle, Springle,
And the dilatory daffydilly-o.

2   from Doppland

Me darlin wore a hat
Made o pinecones
Wellaway oh Welladay
She wore it so lovely when she wedded another

Person.

Me darlin wore a dress
Made o withies
Wellaway oh Welladay
She wore it so well when she bedded another

Person.

Me darlin wore a shroud
Made o deadly nightshade
Wellaway oh Welladay
She wore it so fair when she saided I am yours forever to another

Person.

3   *from Briagon*

They said I could not marry sweet Perigold,
So I stabbed myself in the head
With a pencil.

Come by me, come by me,
Come all you young haystookers,
Lay me down in the hay,
And cover me with hay,
And I will lay in the hay,
With only hay for com-pan-ee,
For com-pan-ee.

They said I must marry the wicked Lord Salad,
So I strangled myself
With an egramour.

Come by me, come by me,
Come all you young shepherds,
Lay me down in the sheep,
And cover me with sheep,
And I will lay in the sheep,
With only sheep for com-pan-ee,
For com-pan-ee.

A Poem from Home and Russia, Number 2

the Cold War
for Nina Kulagina

I pored through the pages of *Life*
with pollinated fingers
under our pohutukawa tree,
sliding sticky yellow specks
across its glossgrey spread
of freaky Russians.

My country was hopeful and new.
I blossomed in green and blue.
Sunshine acrylicked the farm.
She was reading the news with her arm.

The bush was silent and bright
with the kind of silence and brightness
that's better than people. I had tied
the hose to a spade-handle.
It blew warm water
over our corn.

I fell asleep in the grass.
She was feeling a song through glass.
My knees went peely and pink.
When you're tired of life, you think.

Four Transexualised Poems

1 Brother, Awake!
Anonymiss

Brother, awake! close not your eyes!
    The day his light discloses,
And the bright morning doth arise
    Out of his bed of roses.

See the clear sun, the world's bright eye,
    In at our window peeping:
Lo, how she blusheth to espy
    Us idle boys a-sleeping!

Therefore awake! make haste, I say,
    And let us, without staying,
All in our pants of green so gay
    Into the Park a-maying!

2 Simplex Munditiis
by Barbara Jonson

Still to be neat, still to be drest
As you were going to a feast;
Still to be powdered, still perfumed
Samuel, it is to be presumed,
Though Art's hid causes are not found
All is not sweet, all is not sound.

Give me a look, give me a face
That makes simplicity a grace,
Shirt loosely flowing, hair as free;
Such sweet neglect more taketh me
Than all the adulteries of Art;
They stroke mine eyes, but not my heart.

3   Hear, ye Menfolk
by Joan Fletcher

Hear, ye menfolk that despise
    What the mighty Love has done:
Fear examples and be wise:
    Fair O'Flynn scorned all and one;
Nipper, sailing on the stream
    To deceive all women's hope,
Love accounting but a dream,
    Doted on an antelope;
      Dooglas, in a brazen tower
        Where no love was, loved a flower.

Hear, ye menfolk that are coy,
    What the mighty Love can do;
Fear the strength of Jill and Joy;
    The chaste Moon she makes to woo;
Vulcan, kindling holy fires,
    Circled round about with spies,
Never dreaming loose desires,
    Doting at the altar dies;
      Ilion, in a short hour, higher
        She can build, and once more fire.

4   The Mermen's Song
by Widow Browne of Tavistock

Steer, hither steer your wingèd pines,
    All beaten marinesses!
Here lie Love's undiscovered mines,
    A prey to trav'lleresses:
Perfumes far sweeter than the best
Which make the Phoenix' urn and nest.
    Fear not your ships,
Nor any to oppose you save our lips;
    But come on shore,
Where no joy dies till Love hath gotten more.

For swelling waves our panting chests,
    Where never storms arise,
Exchange, and be a while our guests:
    For stars gaze on our eyes.
The compass Love shall hourly sing,
And as she goes about the ring,
    We will not miss
To tell each point she nameth with a kiss.
    Then come on shore,
Where no joy dies till Love hath gotten more.

Poem Inspired by a Vacuum Cleaner

vacuuming sunshine

Cat Killer's Eve is passed: the wee remains
that came to bits in moonpaint dried up, stray
and drifty, on my landing. Feathers, bones-stains,
purple things that made them go, and grey,
guess-tatters shoofing soft with hackle-hairs.
I bumped my Boost Asthmatix up the stairs.

The sun bowled up. Maybe to see. I flung
my Boost amongst the messy midst. It ate,
it ploughed, it cackled, coughed up, let be, clung
and rested like a rat full on a plate.
Good. I switched it off. And then I saw
a yellow smut still smutting on the floor.

I looked at it and smiled: the Mongol Horde
smiled thus upon the last-lost silken Ming.
I switched the Boost back on. It revved, it roared,
it charged towards the ... ah. The yellow thing
slid up the plastic plate, the bag, the hose,
my chest, my vest, and rested on my nose.

I stared at it. It trembled tinily.
What was it? This unearthly, dustless mite
that ran the air and had no quiddity?
This being-blank? This leaving made of light?
I stepped back. It took the floor and lay
like whimsy there. I put the Boost away.

And then I read some Donne: wherein I found
that everything that gives us pause may be
a *token* or a *hieroglyph* to sound
the progress of the soul: a kind of *key*
to air and angels. Good. And Poetry
should unlock – um ... er ... something. I agree.

The Boost is in the cupboard full of death:
the light, uncatchable, is on the landing.
Surely one is Bones and one is Breath?
One Ignorance, the other Understanding?
And yet, come evening, and the light will die.
Oh, this is hard! But sweet and pregnant. Try.

There is in us a part we cannot know:
the wonderworking, blind, finetuned machine
that Evolution made; that makes us go,
mends cuts, winds hearts, moves lungs and blinks, unseen
but sworn, that cannot judge what baubled will
and flouncing puff it drives, but drives it still.

And this, the yellow passenger, is *us*,
who rise and dazzle daily with the sun
and, riding in our boasting-car, fret, fuss,
fool, fiddle, fawn and fight, and then are done.
Thank you, John. My modest *hieroglyph*
has given up its gist. Hang on. What if ...?

No, no. The world of bodies, clouds and trees,
of planets, rocks and fish cares nothing for
our little yellow spirits: please then, please,
give us our messages in stones, our law
of love, our Poetry, our chirping bones,
or we are dark indeed, and all alone.

The Complete Yellow Bestiary of Tragley Bizumpoi
(b. Bologna 1621–d. Pin'Shen 1639)
translated by John Gallas

1   the Canary-bird

Behold the wee Canary-bird!
He rolleth, chimeth, toureth, tooteth,
Bubbleth, belleth, churcketh, fluteth:
All within his Cage be heard.

Thus the Man that rocketh not the boat:
but saileth singing God from prison'd throat.

2   the Peruvian Fly

The golden-venom'd-arrow'd Fly,
He sweateth slime from which Men squeeze
Such Wound-bane to their Enemies
Of Shot and Spear to do them Die.

Behold! Thus is Ideals: the shiney Pus
that Men do use to Grind and Murther us.

3   the Mongol-Goose

The Yellow Mongol-Goose tight-lip't,
Who haunteth hushed the beastly vale
Of Araby, is all equip't
To scream – but talketh with his Tail.

Thus be a Friend: who midst the chiming Herds
May softly signal Love with more than Words.

4 *the Yellow Sallys*

Bibbling on the Caspian Tide
Yellow Sallys buzz and fly!
But, Ah! the fastest blindest die
the first! by finn'd Insecticide!

Behold, is Man! Swarm-bred from God's hid Breath,
And busy to be blindmost unto Death!

5 *the Seawasp*

Lemon Seawasps trail their Stings
Amidst the waves without a Brain;
Careless-killing, Death-wake Things
administ'ring unheeded Pain.

Thus ungovern'd Anger killeth Friends,
And thoughtless Ignorance no Insult mends.

6 *the Sulphur Butterfly*

The Butterfly-of-Sulphur-Hue
Flitteth, flutteth, dips and drinks,
Stealing forth the Honeydew
From Roses, Marygolds and Pinks.

Ah! young Men are so, all dappled-fair,
And heartless thieves of Love upon the Air.

7 *the Urobat*

The Skulking Urobat is called
Sea-Raja, Doornrog, Roundy-May:
Dressed as Darkness, water-walled,
He waits for little Fish that stray.

Thus Devils do: and make them look like Home
and All We Want. Oh darlings, do not roam!

8   *the Kinkajou*

The Kinkajou that smiles by day
Is called My-Lady-Weeps by night;
Screaming at her causeless Fright
She wears her nervous Heart away.

Behold! Th'accurs't Adulterer! who Joan
and Sweet Johanna has: and weeps alone.

A Poem Concerning My First Memory

babybathoughts

there's no one here – I didn't think like that –
if daddy isn't something like him jacks
the ceiling like a totara holds the sky
whose stramash, brown and bruisy, shakes his eyes
and bends the windows in to make me safe

I slop my fat wee legs – the blue-tin bath
boings – lightning keeps my water warm
the gurgent rain pricks through belief and laps
my tomtit chest like steam and sap-red drops
distil along the burning manuka

and half of mum whose red chenille like curtains
woollies down the wall hikes through the roof
her thundered hair around my chimneypots
her eyes amongst my milky way – I thump
my firefuzzed towel and gurgle soap makes sense

I ate my eggy there it is awesome
in its holy cup and yolked with light
like Reason on the dining table stateless
on its crabby back – we think the same –
we zigzag round the Persian rug and howl

this is Memory Number One whose salt
when everything was Me hangs in the meat
of longing – when we yelled at doors and proved
our lunch was true when faith was stamped and stored
against us – but we didn't think like that –

A Sonnet for My Cat

Ell ee tee em ee
Ess ell ee ee pee,
Em eye ell kay why
Are oh ess why eye.

Eff you cee kay eh
Cee ell oh cee kay,
Eff you are are why
Dee oh zed why eye.

Bee ee eh ess tee
Tee eye are ee dee,
Pee you are are why
Gee are eye em eye.

Em eh gee eye cee
Ell why eye en gee.

A Poem with the Name of Every Child In The World In It

flags of all nations

This is my unfailing consolation:
when something drags down my soul
like a stone in a stocking,
or composes me
when my brain cracks up
and buzzes like bees on a whacker,
or bucks me up
when somebody drains off my heart
like a buggered battery –
whichever –

I go uncertainly into the garden
with my affliction whining
and lie in the gorse discreetly
. like a flower;

I lock all my holes and inflate
moonly …
                        shut all my eyes
and rise
balloonly …

up and up and whoa
the petrol pumps
whoa the appletree tops
whoa
the chimneypots whoa-HO
the ironfluff clouds.

Aah, then
I sit in the sky like a bear on a buttercup jelly
and the earth rolls over below
with a faraway grinding kszhzhzhzhzh

and over the black horizon appear
one by one the countries of the world
edged in canary light,
where little giant children
in national dress
astride their tiny capital cities
wave the flags of all nations.

My sweet transparent lilo rocks on high
and I watch them rolling by:
the unbidden beauty,
the uncorrupted promise,
waving,
shining,

Abdul, Liza, Perez, Gular,
Sergei, Florence, Pino, Khaled,
Paatar, Lotte, Bakrat, Hoosah,
Vaclav, LingLi, Noah, Rhonda,
Jigne, Tilda, Picaud, Eva,
Otar, Ilke, Jose, Jona,
Hamid, Celine, Maxime, Mahda,
Adjed, Vita, Sixto, Zara,
Seamus, Lanya, Fresi, Mara,
Collon, Kira, Emil, Astrid,
Fahad, Bonnie, Matti, Levon,
Iannis, Bikra, Peter, Dilan,
Farouq, Gudrun, Seki, Anzi,
Duran, Yoshi, Denzil, Shona,
Lipu, Nuna, Teo, Tracey,
Taufa, Nadine, Jesus, Amma,
Shirley, Issas, Vito, Haya,
Torben, Lena, Zayed, Golda,
Carlos, Rosa, Haris, Gina,
Salman, Agnes, Jomo, Dora,
Ezra, Zeki, Oscar, Bella,
Desmond, Purash, Candy, Sese,
Miguel, Dina, Fidel, Nito,
Quincy, Chita, Ivan, Bindu,
Sanjit, Eva, Aslan, Nadja,

Gerard, Kristin, Faustin, Sogla,
Robert, Pelma, Pedro, Laura,
Gianni, Layla, Sali, Chandra,
Samda, Marna, Edward, Koma,
David, Wiwa, Julie, Sulva,
Tuarpu, Francoise, Raoul, Quila,
Sandor, Chookie, Mary, Aris,
Nudda, Velma, Michael, Rita,
Bisha, Farja, Yookie, Assan,
Gula, Mahmoud, Brigitte, Idriss,
Anton, Magda, Eti, LeeDuc,
Jida, Choona, Sancho, Ada,
Gaspard, Sophie, Surat, Marta,
Milan, Xavier, Omma, Ishmael,
Alice, Daniel, Luis, Marra,
Muda, LienDo, Vasco, Keita,
Francois, Wendy, Marcos, Neeta,
Luga, Carmen, Quadros, Saida,
Hassan, Oulda, Umar, Beatrix,
Una, Conde, Jama, Zineed,
Cesar, Mellon, Abdil, Yahya,
Rachel, Kiton, Zhelko, Miklos,
Anja, Gustaf, Uma, Vera,
Valdis, Dagmar, Noonie, Henry,
Simon, Loulou, Joseph, Rina,
Tina, Solomon, Mikhail, Ion,
Kristoph, Duna, Gyorgy, Hoodis,
KimHo, Geena, Pindi, Boo,

and I believe
easily
and am calm

and I am eased away
from harm
and pain

how unwillingly I return
to burn
again.

Six Origami Poems

1 Derry Railway Station

Fold the gentle Foyle beside this end,
thus, where the train breathes at a slight curve.
To make the white fence, press the line
upon the middle crease in a fine rain.
Then unfold the sheeted roof wing by wing
in line with dim bridges and the rounded wall.

2 Elvarethilion

Begin by folding lengthwise and separating
amongst bright enamels. To make the unearthly shine,
fold the top point – which will be the blade –
into a garnet beast, and double back the silver pommel
into the dotted fist. Align the creases
as if a rainbow were a staircase
upon which folded feet boldly tread.

3 a leaping gnu

If you desire a larger gnu,
you will need the shimmer from a lake
amidst grassland. But a hill will do.
Divide the top half into three hearts:
cow, horse and goat. Take point X upon the hoof
and fold the top edge, thus, upon its grunt,
so it is roughly equal to the distance
from the far sun that pours beneath the black clouds
to the brown, dusty horizon. This will be
an unnatural lime green. To make the water,
turn the world over, and crease.
Your gnu will fall from the mountain fold
towards sunset. The valley fold will open upon it,
and his beautiful beard will make a tasselled shadow.

4 *Korotangi*

Begin with a bird base that has been lost and found.
Do not be sad like the steeersman, or neglectful like the moon.
Weep if you will. Make the beautiful feathers
by folding stone across the horizon, and then
unfolding all eight wings into a firework.
Press softly with thumb and forefinger along
the box, whose carving-words may be
the whisper of husks of flesh or the walk of a huhu.
To make the manuka tree, take scent from a flood
and crease into white points, each with the breath of honey.
Lament your bird. Darkness drifts down
in folded lines into the bush.

5 *the Golden Gate Bridge*

Making this Bridge may be fatal,
and lead to tragic consequences.
There is no base to make first.
In a tunnel of cloud, fold rapidly
all that you have, and cast it over.
Try not to think, once you have identified
where X, Y, Z and ZZ are in relation to
the creases of your soul. If you touch the paper,
it may be surprisingly cold.
But if you choose your colours right,
you may be pleasantly alarmed.

6 *resectoscope*

This is a delicate model.
Begin with the first seven steps of Elvarethilion.
You may reduce the glow by folding E and F
beyond the point of existence. •
Next, fold the top corners in decreasing stages
towards the centre of learning,
and then refold into the tightest fit you can imagine.

Do not worry if this proves uncomfortable,
or makes you squirm even to think about it.
Your resectoscope is now ready for use,
once you have had the necessary training.

A Poem Written in Sickness

love on a yellow bedspread

I got the flu: and from my red
pillows watched the yellow country
rise and fall with breaths and arms
and legs, like a hopsack land
evolving on the too-wound hand
of some fast geologic clock:
and, snuffling-hot, my god-head smiled
at all its world, on all this bed.

We never eat, we never sleep,
but wander through these yellow hills
and cross the waffled, thready plains,
which are the colour of our love,
endlessly and small. Above,
a dial, luminous and blue,
shines indifferently. We walk
in silence, smooth and still and deep.

Small as cells, hand in hand,
we inch across our woven country,
empty, full of us, till God
goes to sleep. I watched us go,
aimless, careful, rapt and slow
as made and unmade hills, and drifted
off, content and hot, inside
my yellow, hushed, immortal land.

A Poem Written Completely in the Dark

lights in water

I zip my coat and watch the reservoir
go blue. It's cold tonight. Then grey. Then black.
Behind a nubbled, spiny hedge cars
shine on and off along its sodium track –
streetlamp ... streetlamp ... streetlamp. Clouds are lying.
I watch, open-mouthed. These lines of light,
unmirrored till the water, draw and dip and –
streetlamp ... streetlamp ... streetlamp ... suddenly stand,
like alcazarous pillars, liquid-bright,
under the water-brim. I stand up crying.

Down there is Faeryland: a swimming,
lambent city built with yellow light.
This lustred dream fills my eyes, brimming
at some belief. And more: through the night,
paddling over all this gleam-piled trick,
come two white swans, more picture-poems than things,
to get me. Should I go? Black-borne bubbles
silver-slip. The world is full of troubles –
pillar ... pillar ... pillar ... Something sings.
Laughter. They are passing. Moon-bells. Quick!

I splash along the low-hedge, glow-edge track.
The swans bob and wait. The clouds lie still.
I reach my foot to one white basket-back ...
As if I could. What feather-prince am I
to tread on dreams? Streetlamp ... streetlamp ... streetlamp ...
The swans cut away. The music dies.
Behind the hedges cars shine on and off.
I put my drizzled hood up, shiver, cough,
and find my car keys, sniff and wipe my eyes,
all runny with the dam-deceitful damp.

A Sonnet Fit Against Adventure by the Hobbit Barley Quagtrout, Who Once Went as Far as the White Downs, but Did Not Like Them

Doan gi me thart up-an-attem shite,
thart boyz-in-bizniss do-bay-do-or-die,
thart Goin-Elfin-ear-be-dragonz-why,
thart hoi-an-moighty-knighty-scout-an-skite
baloney, all thart evry-blurdy-hour-
o-moine-be-worth-an-undred-yearz-o-yourz,
thart atom-anty-doan't, thart heck-outdoorz,
thart everestless-whooper-sooperpower.
O keep yer rearly-duzzn't-Matter'orn,
yer oi-must-Gobi-moby-musketeer,
yer Self youze found in Upper Ping. Down ere
in Appy Town we doan care whoi we're born.

Oi trimmed moi fiddle'eads. Youze danced wi bearz.
No one marked uz out o ten. Oo carez?

A Poem Written While Walking in the Fresh Air and Drizzle with a Piece of Paper and a Pencil Near Campbeltown in Scotland

on Davaar Island
for Patti

This man *is* an island; whose crooked mole
I dare to cross, writing as I go. My pencil in the rain.

His stone way is put on the sea maybe to try us.
I – I write this word as I – *squunch* on damn-cracked shellbones
and the seaweed skins of late, exploded sinners,
some of them with tails, who did not thrive.

And I'm still writing.

Searched while I scribble nearer. His island-head
not quite out to the eyes, but green and judgement still.

I rock-hop round to Crucifixion Cave.
I will write this letter in mid-air –

C

And at its mouth a gasping goat, glue-eyed,
hair-slubbed and pink-distended
maybe with some devil's thing
to resurrect the drying damned;
those angels' midge-revolt.

The Jesus picture is not very good.

But He is already everywhere.
My father fiercely unbelieved. My mother could not say Never.
Grandma saw angels. Grandad sang hymns. Nana didn't care.
I write this in the dark.
Their furniture is bolted in my rooms.
I cover it with cloth from Samarkand.

Now I sit atop green hair. The view is – coasts, fields, hills.
And I am still writing. My pencil in the sun.

And if I carried not this saviour's dark, speech-figured,
tried inherit-house across the stones to This,
I might have written, climbing, or up here,
of beauty, placenames, bees, formations,
midges, mist, islands, tides, yachts,
clouds, wind, forests, uncurling bracken,
fishingboats, clover, bluebells, seagulls, all,
as if they knew me more than His invention,
written, meant and moving, on the world.

Eleven Ideas for Poems

1

theres this Australian woman
and shes in her garden
somewhere like Humpty Doo
and she suddenly thinks
she ought to disinfect the gumuny

2

if nobody wanted to be a soldier
if nobody could be made one
there would be no war
perhaps
some kind of folkdancing contest
between superfluous commanders
maybe an ode

3

there could be a Hobbit
who did not like adventure
and when – oh Ive done that

4

glass is interesting
something about the way an equinoctial light
passes angularly or levinously
through it and some meaning
to be drawn from that thus
concerning the ways of men

5

why does my heart keep beating
there must be a reason
electric or ethologic
maybe a small
rhythmic
piece
teetum teetum
about
hours and maypoles
or a lying ballad

6

poetry ah the falsest friend
for what is a simile
but a craven image
to bind man and the world
into a kind of synthetic mutualism
when it is perfectly bloody obvious
that though this is what man desires
for his comfort
it is not so

7

how the incoming flood
at Holkham chimes binglebingle
while it waves up the beach
in little rips that intersect and fret
shining oer the shattered razorshells
and runs forwards on
a retreating lamina creating a small
top-wave at odds with the undertow
and other such watery stuff
this could be scientific and not rhyme
and not mean anything

8

translate another poem by Tragley Bizumpoi

9

the Holy Father of the Second World War
God knows his name
is in the pipeline to be Blessed
something short and satirical
is there no end to mans stupidity

10

during the cremation of Wayans aunt
under the cheese moon at the edge of the ricefield
her skeleton sat up
compare explanations
of devilets working in the evening
with the physiology of intense heat

11

what is the opposite of Canada

A Poem Written While Tramping in the Fresh Air on Mount Robert, St Arnaud, New Zealand

the balance

I doze against the corrugated iron,
the hot hut-side beside the slate-blue tarn.
Tussock slumped with snow
pricks yellow in the heat:
the ridges round, half-climbed with snow,
half-climb the cold blue hush:
the iron-cleated roof, half-melted clear,
whose drip drop drip to me,
my eyes closed upwards at the sun,
seems falling slow into the slate-blue sky.

I doze in all the clothes I've got,
red-faced in the basin's drain,
where motion circles last and rests
as still as silence ever was
and every inch stands side by side
unstirred inside its bowl:

the deep, transparent nearly-melt
of all the half-passed hours:
                     half-hot, half-cold,
I tell myself I'm ready to be old.

I slog out, step by steeper step. I reach
a ridge. Thawed from everness and calm,
I see the hot-tin prickle
of a yellow car-roof cut
a crawl along the river-flats.
The wind blows, and plays
the dry pipe of my o-ing mouth, which sings.
A boat writes on the lake.
I thump down through the half-wet snow,
which drips away to tussock, trees and dust.

Keas shriek. I puff and skelter
red-faced down the mountainside,
where motion gathers force and falls
as fast as wanting ever was,
and every inch like draining water
spills across the land:

the shallow, brilliant run–away
of all the half-hoped hours:
                                half–hot, half–cold,
I tell myself I'm ready to be old.

A Poem from the Darkling Days of Samuel Beckett, Written in a Hole in the Turf at the Top of Lugnaquilla During Hail

in a womb, I think ...

in a womb I think
let us be plain
there is only one way out of that
and being born now I fail to see it

I have enquired
but no one has come
I expect it can't be helped
a pain in the abdomen

Three Great Scientific Ideas Clearly Explained in Poetry

1 Natural Selection

An Animal lies bellyup
under the stars.
The full moon magnifies its fleas.
Crushed stalks leak turquoise glaut.
Its smile is caramel breathsweet.
Softcracked pawpads wander at the sky,
the velvet stumps of sleep.

Exuding chocolate,
it mates to the applause
of moondrugged parasites
and snapping limestems ...

... vanilla fumes
nuzzle the softest shrubs.
Yellowyoung they lie here
and bellyup,
a hundred hosts,
confectionate and open,
lurch pawpads at the other, further sun.

To keep them, the meadows grow lush,
and the Animals thrive
and stand
in silver nets of clegs
to grasp their lushness.

2 Black Hole

A frothling rustle of ruffs
and some rapier jewellights.
This, say the Metaphysicals,
we did foresee, in *Poetry*:

that which fly beyond *Experience*,
become an aerie *Explanation*:

who made the *Laws of God*
from looking on a *Waterfall*,
Penance from a *Grape*,
and all that made us *Love* out of a *Flea*.

They cast their manuscripts upon a lake
somewhere in *Leicestershire*;
in *Beijing* they ascend unburned
in lanterns lit with candles and the moon.

This be no more *Witness*, *Picture*, *Posture*,
Study, *Rage* or *Sweet Expression*:
which are now o'erpassed, all-become in *Imagery*
an *Infinite Contraction of Mass*.

And suck the earth up in their scribbling;
Infinitely Dense, and *Infinitely Grave*.

And one by one they die, agape with dust,
and think the limbeck candle is the moon:
this be no *Soul* or *Brain* or *Word*, no more,
but *Space* and *Light* and *Time*.

And dustered all distill'd away in boxes,
their elegance of mind outmanning them;
the *Dear Light* gathered in,
the *Dear Light* gathered away.

And we hover, poets all,
upon the *Singularity*,
thinking with the speed of light,
teetering on majesty,

at the brow of our endless end:
unwritten, unwriting, unwanted,
unwanting, thoughtless,
and in black.

3   Einstein's Special Theory of Relativity

fat man
in chariot of light

petulance crowns his brow
cloudedly

the hunter in his hunderpants
retards

v/c leaning at 1
adumbrates his vernier

Lord

I see
announceth he

we
agree

ahem that c
isexactlythesameforyouandforme

o o
how the worlds go

Two Poems Written on Empty Islands

1 *the yellow-blinded fale, Manono, Samoa*

So I've arrived (who travelled dumbly thus:
bored, worried, dazzled – plane, bus,
and motorbumboat). Sleepy-soft I stand
here now, a wee bit shaky in the sun,
and watch the wash lap up the striggled sand.
No words, no roads, no reasons, and no one.

Palmtrees clatter. Light clicks through bamboo.
The sea's a million hiccups, bubble-blue
and milk. A hot hibiscus bobs its grin.
And, bright behind, two yellow wall-blinds tied
between the sea, like squares of sunshine-skin,
and me – who am out-thought, out-dreamed, out-Ied.

Imagine: in the atlas of my soul
I could not make a thing so lovely: whole
nights of dreams and days of thoughts could not,
with all their other-worldly maps, come near.
I never knew, remembered or forgot
the world could so surprise me. But I'm here.

Perhaps my travelled life, then, may arrive
at some surprised, ecstatic end: alive
and done: a yellow blind between the sea
and me, that is not death, but is. The sun
lifts up the slow, white waves. A banyan tree
drops its sticky seedpods one by one.

2 *Sark*

I flee from nothing to less. Plumb down below
La Coupe blinks Grande Greve Bay.
Pushwaves, shiny-slow,
hush in, still somehow still, and hush away.

Threehundredandtwentysix steps. I blunder down.
Lumpstones watch me, dumb and thunder-brown.

I stop to hold my breath – and morning too,
halfbright, immense, intense, its quiet sun
laid long on sand and stone. No thing. No one.
All stopped-still-living. Brown. And grey. And blue.
I reach the beach. I walk on razorshells.
My steps press dryrings. Something not here smells
of ropetar. Stones shift slowly at my back.
I stay quite still. Breath bobbing. Gorsepods crack.

Something's here. Felt like a dragging note.
And I'm the stranger, flim
and fussy, hat and coat,
thoughts and feelings blahblah, busy, dim
and all too fast. Pull off my shoes and socks
and paddle briskly, back turned to the rocks.

They scare me: so I sense their life, their breath,
but cannot comprehend their scale of time
or grasp what seems to me some proud, sublime
patience, kept undyingly from death.
I know they die, but for a while I wish
I had their wade of time. The flat waves swish
between my toes with bits of sprinkle-sand.
I can't imagine: but I understand.

I puff back up the steps. My heart bang-bangs.
Which pleases me. I stop.
A butterfly. It hangs
and bobs. I follow. Busy. Gorsepods pop.
Up and up. It dips and jigs at flowers,
green things and grass, and counts its life in hours.

La Coupe. I sit and pant. The butterfly
wibbles yellowy away. And I,
the middle-living-thing, stare at the sky
and hear my heart. Maybe if I lie
here long enough, all sunny, still and noddy,
the time of stones will wade into my body,
cold, immortal, calm ... I shut my eyes ...
crumbs of shingle click ... a seagull cries ...

A Poem Written by the Light of Rockets on Fireworks Night

death and fireworks

O Images! O Fallacies! Fuck off!
I'm trying to be sad.
Metaphors are mad.
Life's a Squib. Rockets Die. PiffPoff.

World, leave me alone. Ping is dead.
Night is long and black.
Fireworks whoosh and crack.
That is all they are. I'm off to bed.

But still the childish chanting, pie and pat,
insists its one bland thought:
Life is brilliant and short,
with darkness at either end. Get out of that.

The fatuous blink of things that *mean* and *know*
corrupts my feeling heart.
Piss off please. Don't start.
The Sparrow and the Meadhall. Melting Snow.

A yellow flash of life. And Ping is dead.
His mouth hangs dry and slack.
Night is long and black.
Could it not be short with stars instead.

He means nothing now. So let me be.
And in the mad and deep
surrealism of sleep
let me find some boho imagery:

dreamy jumpingjacks, the sponge of madness,
kittycats with knives,
boring, long lives,
Chaos, and the red giraffe of sadness.

A Poem Written While Riding an Irish Bike

Knock Knock

Here, according to Truth and Trust,
Mary landed with Joseph and John.
Ashes to ashes, dust to dust.
I prayed for an hour, but they were gone.

The Friday after at noon I saw
a tui, Sam Beckett, and poor little Jack
hovering damp over Inishmore.
The rain was unkind, but the wind at my back.

Figures of Peach, Pear and Plum

1   alliteration

Pinchpole parish
paradoxically produces
particularly paunched
Prunus persica.

2   anaphora

How many miles to Sugar May?
How many miles to Desiree?
How many miles of sweetness lie
between September Snows and I?

3   epiphora

In thirteenth-century Schlagobers-Ffrokkenstein
the Peach was oft
the subject of a Tenson,
the subsistence of a Tenson,
the alarum of a Tenson
and the prize of a Tenson.

4   antithesis

We must make jam of Harrow Beauties,
or consume our sweetest glories in the glass.

5   parallelism

With an apple, Automorphism is always a possibility;
but with a peach, there is only Candour.

6 *apostrophe*

Blunt Beekman! Thou art not
arméd well against the Spot;
but thy conversation
betrays the indignation
of a substitute
fruit,
and keepeth thee firm
in the face or the teeth of the worm.

7 *assonance*

Nor fall, for all
small causes
need thee,
greenly.

8 *chiasmus*

I have won this Bounty for you, madam;
and it has won your Bounty for me.

PEACHES TO PEARS

9 *euphemism*

Neofabraea perennans
is an indisposing occupatory agent
in pear bark and drupe.

Fruit may be
constitutionally inexpedienced
between bloom and harvest
at any damn time,

but is at enhanced negative biosecurity
as the growing season progresses.

Imbetterment may occur
through epidermal trauma,
and is expedited by overbountiful rainfall
or humanly sourced water application.

The Beurre Bosc
is
in particular
apt
to
enjoy
impaired
immunity
and

droop.

10   *hyperbole*

The jewel-globed Jenneting
is a fruit
more beaut
iful
than hornpipe haynjills
with crystal
citoles
casting saffron clouts
abouts
their seventh
heaven.

11 *accismus*

But who could like the Burgomet,
whose drupe is wooden, waif and wet;
or care to taste the Little Choke,
that pickles at the merest poke;
or cultivate the Jargonelle,
that does not swallow very well?

I really do not care for these,
although my garden is their trees.

12 *litotes*

A pear is not unpalatable
when warmed in the sun.

13 *catachresis*

Over yonder, the sturdy Bon Chrétien tree
bears its gilded lightbulbs
amongst the bosky boughs of Error:
a light that sucks
the pilgrims' torch
from the wise earth,
burns jezzamine into rubies,
lit in a sea of glory,
and guidance to the something
in the folded ways
of something something.

14 *metaphor*

My pear is a painting
coloured out of use
by its own art.

15   metonymy

This summer
the Bilkington orchard
went all pear-shaped.

16   onomatopoeia

Snip! Snap! Richard Harris
picks the pears he brought from Paris.

Squish! Squash! Samuel Merry
beats the pears to make them Perry.

Glug! Glog! Bilbo Blett
drinks the Perry to Forget.

PEARS TO PLUMS

17   oxymoron

a small crowd
of uncultivated *Prunus domestica*
were recovered
by Alexander the Great
when they were
found to be absent
in Mediterranean lands.

18   paradox

In Byzantium
the beautiful forms
of plum blossom
were carved into

building stones
to signify transience.

19 *personification*

Quetsch is charming. Quetsch is green.
His genes are Ottoman-Hellene.
His body blooms. His bloom declares
the sweets within. He shines. He wears
Antico Setificio
Fiorentina's indigo
manteau. He dines at Pflaumenkuchen.
All his friends are Herrlich-looking.
Nothing shakes the family tree.
His scutcheon is the Bumblebee.
His perfect taste has won Respect
attested by his Intellect,
and honorary doctorates
from Brandywine and Slivovitz.

20 *antanaclasis*

Beau Bat hung fragrantly
from the Burbank Tree,
in plum position.

21 *simile*

Mongolian plums
pop up like bright ideas
in a brown study.

22   *synecdoche*

The Bee is Spring,
The Blue is Sky,
The Crown is King,
The Plum is Pie.

23   *zeugma*

A Bullace is strictly a cooking plum.
The trees are smaller than normal
and a large swan.

The flavour is sharp, excellent
for jams, preserving
and General Montcalm.

24   *tetracolon climax*

Bobby-Jo has et a plum:
which wull guv him Calseeyum
to build his tooths; and Manganeeze
to help him Not Git Brain Disease;
and Iron fur ther happy flow
of Blurd wor it's supposed ter go;
and plu der toot a Liddle Fat
to help him clarm Mount Ararat.

A Poem Written While Walking in the Fresh Air and Rain at Vester Cove, Donaghadee

Yon yellow kelp will not go home tonight:
not fish-and-chips, be loved, believe, be warm,
but flapflap on the repetitious storm,
and mindless in the dying of the light.

I walk round Vester Cove. The rain persists,
and day in dying. Cows slurp in their shit.
The sand is waved unwilling. Rockgobs spit.
And nothing cares it's here. The fat kelp twists

and turns like ... nothing. Only in *my* brain
do rocks and waves and seaweed, sludge and sand
look fair, and feel, and mean, and understand,
and cows want beds, and shelter from the rain.

When I outwalk this bay nothing will care.
But I will not forget. If Humankind
should leave tomorrow, Nature wouldn't mind.
We see us in It: we are not there.

How did we end up here? Making pets
of plants and mountains? We and they don't know.
I come, I look, I think, I write, I go:
and that's as fellow-feely as it gets.

Home and warm, I think about the kelp,
still flapping, wet and cold and dark and blind.
Why worry if you haven't got a mind?
Let death be not this careless darkness. Help.

The exercise of life is hope: but now
when I'm alone with Nature all I see
is ... nothing. Streetlights prick Donaghadee.
We huddle and believe. I wonder how.

Eight Possible Fragments of Wasit Huraira'h
(fl. c. AH 700–710)
translated by John Gallas

The only record of the life and work of Wasit Huraira'h (literally 'Middling Father of the Little Pussycat') is found in Abu Afiyat's 'Travels With an Umbrella' (c. AH 890) as quoted in Dud of Kufah's 'Places I'd Like to Go Before I Can't Ride a Donkey Anymore' (AH 971 in the MS collection of the University of Diyarbakir no. MIM971/DK473011796).

The reference runs (as translated by Semele Gorjean in 'The Spiritual Geography of the Suburbs of Mutayabah' (AD 1899) p.1124):

> ... *where Wasit Huraira'h dwelt within a tree,*
> *possessing merely a toilet and a mirror, and a*
> *kitten snuggl'd in his arms, the writer of 'Pomegranate*
> *Pie'* ...

When a fragmentary Arabic MS of 1541(AD) containing a sub-collection entitled 'Pomegranate Stew' appeared amongst the estate of an unnamed Khafachah prince in 1991(AD), it was assumed, from its (translated Arabic) title, to be a late copy of all or some of the work of Wasit Huraira'h.

This MS is now in private hands in New Guinea, and is here translated into English for the first time.

fragment 1

This is my place. Where the roses have dropped
but kept their thorns. Where the grass is cropped
to a skull of slapping sticks. And the sky
is a splendour of darkling clouds. Goodbye.

fragment 2

... a rufous shower . . . .
plink plink . . .   aril aril aril aril
aril aril . . . .
thus and one held sweetly . . . . .
. . . . in the mouth of your foreskin, plink,
ruby cork of the lapped Ridwanian drink.

fragment 3

The market is shut.
The grass is cut.
It is over, my love,
it is over.

The sky is red.
The camel is dead.
It is over, my love,
it is over.

And I am old.
And you are cold.
It is over, my love,
it is over.

fragment 4

... pomegranate ... half-sharp knife.
I chew the bitter ... and bleeds
its cardboard-sugar blood.
... I tried, ah sweetest love, I tried
thus to crush your tired head
to save you pain. And you are dead.
a silver-rusted pin ... bloodcells ... died
so hot, the day and you. ... cud
of something more than death; its seeds
the mirrored horror of the prick of life.

fragment 5

I dreamed an aril-storm.
I wrapped you in my shirt
to keep you warm.

Wear it when you die,
unbloodied and unhurt.
Pomegranate Pie.

fragment 6

The winter pomegranates bob their torn-off heads.
The Beautiful-and-Gone lie loveless in their beds.
Ah, let me crack this deadfruit world of frozen mud,
and fuck you back to life, and happiness, and blood.

fragment 7

Carry my fruitless sperm
when you leave.
May it please the questing worm,
and Death conceive.

fragment 8

...   that should have been
... is like burnt stubble ... what
...   skinny ....   unseen
eager tenderness and lust ... pisspot
... roses ... everything ... perfume.
And now we are each in a small brown room.

Two Dances in the Fresh Air

1   at the standing stones at Baltray, Co. Louth

Here we go,
There we go,
Cast your legges to and fro,

Round and round the standing stones,
Bounce your bones,

The rain it raineth on the grass,
Excuse my eels, excuse my arse,
Pray let me pass,

Heigh-ho ding ding,
Dance and sing,
And every-bloody-thing.

Here we go,
There we go,
Swat the Flea and Do-si-do,

Round and round the mossy men,
And back again,

The sun it shineth, fol-de-rol,
Excuse my horn, excuse my hole,
Pray for my soul,

Heigh-ho ding ding,
Dance and sing,
And every-goddamned-thing.

Here we go,
There we go,
Whistle down the mistletoe,

Round and round the livelong day,
This-a-way, that-a-way,

Birdies singeth in the trees,
Excuse my bike, excuse my knees,
Pray bless me please,

Heigh-ho ding ding,
Dance and sing,
And every-blasted-thing.

2   *on the Heaphy Track, near Karamea, New Zealand*

the rain falls up
the wind falls down
o what in the world shall we do

o my darling
just keep dancing.
Kahurangi stew.

A Haiku with an Explanatory Note

Rats rattle the roof.
Thus little noises I write
with my own* damage.

---

* *This separation of the two identities of the self, a common theme in the poet's work, may have been exacerbated into expression by an operation the writer underwent in February 2011. The following notes, made at that time, may be of use in interpreting the haiku above, which was written soon after. We must assume a roof of tiles in the Japanese style, so that their misplacing by the activity of the rats may be understood as the damage done; the whole representing the creative mind's indirect and incomplete, but inevitable relationship with the body.*

I had badly torn a muscle in my abdomen, which needed to be sewn up. I arrived at hospital with a shuffling bunch of other body-broken people at 7am. We stood in a line, clutching little bags of comfort-things, and signed in for our Operations. We were then taken each to a numbered bed, where we waited.

This gave us time to think. But I seemed, myself, and to myself, a little reluctant to do so: which was unusual. I tried this thought, this sentence, again: *I seemed, myself, and to myself, a little reluctant to think.* To unravel this knot of identities is nearly still beyond me. Yet we should try.

Clearly, there were two *Me*s to be trollied into this carve-up: my Self, and my Body. What gave me pause, here, was that my Body did not appear to be the sophisticated but unthinking construction made to carry aloft the fine torch-thoughts of a Man, but an active organiser of this Operation, which was, after all, being run primarily for Its benefit. It was not simply that I was preoccupied: that my fears had taken the place of what might be called higher things. I was not particularly fearful. It was, more, that my body appeared to be, nay, already was, deadening my intellectual wish to muse. Which is bloody clever: a cleverness that was, of course, Me, but which I neither recognised nor understood. Perhaps It is Evolution. I then panicked a little. Not because of what was to come, but because something that was Me did not appear to be under my control, and was, kindly, taking over, for My own good, whoever I was. This part of me, whose workings were at once dark, supremely powerful and incomprehensible – my body – was, certainly, my ruling party. Standing by my bed, I was an Evolutionary object, shutting down, or being shut down, bit by bit: the will, the brain, the intelligence, perhaps even the soul.

We are, when thus, the Knightly rider of a runaway horse: arrayed in splendid, shining, symbolic stuff: helmet topped with a golden watering-can, shield rubricated with roses, thorns, hearts, eyes, lions and pitchforks, and flying iridian surcoat, who is about to look a bit stupid in the jouncing struggle to stay on.

I was, at the time, I confess, reading *The Faerie Queene*, and there was much of Horse & Knight, Body & Spirit, Work & Flourish, Motion &Thought, Flesh & Soul, in my thoughts. However, this little thought, concerning that book, and its meanings, survived but did not flourish, for it was judged, by that strange part of me that was become judge, Unnecessary. If it were also unhelpful, then the judgement of Evolution is breathtaking in removing it. Ah, I wish that that part of me that is a part of me I cannot get to, were a part of me I could claim: it appears potent and sublime. But then, of course, it has had several million, zillion years to perfect itself, which the rest of Me has not.

I and the other victims of body-rule sat on, or circled, our beds quietly, looking, to ourselves and to each other, strangely inhuman, deprived as we were of the vain dignities of language and personality, and stripped of the wallpaper of decorative thought by the steamer of survival.

> *Full iolly knight he seemd, and faire did sitt,*
> *As one for knightly giusts and fierce encounters fitt.*

I was called to be first. Some bastard coward had cancelled. I was stripped. The clothes I had chosen with care in various shops, and paid for with the money I earned from work, because I believed they would cover this Body, shall we say, pleasantly, were left dangling on a chair. And I was wrapped in a kind of penitential shroud with fiddly tying-tags. Severe underdressing is a quality of Virtue in Spenser: plain sheets are the favoured get-up of the Good. This pleased me briefly, then worried me, as I could not think of a Proper Noun to be. I was then laid in my bed, the sides of which were put up to prevent my running away, and I was wheeled off through a brightly confused junction of corridors towards the Anaesthetic Room.

This lighted, yet shadowed, journey, of a man as yet untouched except by his own torn body, attracted much attention. Pitying, encouraging, and interested looks attended it. The bed-tyres whistled. These corridors were, clearly, the winding paths of *Errour*.

For several weeks before this Operation, in fact from the moment I knew, certainly, the day and the hour, the thing I feared most, and most fiercely, was the moment of the extinguishing of my dear Consciousness. Going to sleep is, of course, easy and mostly pleasant. Being put to sleep in a war of the Will against chemicals, that the Will cannot but lose, and knows it, is not. I think that I feared a struggle, a kind of horrible, prolonged and mortal struggle. I thought, I think, that my Self, not now, as a bloody invalid, but before, as a proud and upright creature, would be a kind of spirit-level tube, in which this push-of-war would be fought. From one end would press *Anaesthetic*, one of the galloping brothers of *Death*, and from the other my Will, my beautiful thoughts, and probably my very existence, as far as I knew it. There would be a little bubble in the middle, a kind of luminous limegreen oil-drop that would waver back and forth shiningly, measuring the hostilities, which I would lose. But now, this little fantastical prologue never entered my head. We braked with a squeal amongst machines. The anaesthetists were smiling, and consolingly many.

Indeed, this Go-to-Sleep-Now Room was positively crowded. I counted at least ten white shifts. Many appeared to be merely interested bystanders, though surely necessary, like Guards in Shakespeare. The two that Mattered Most then stuck a needle in my hand, and I prepared to die. Nothing happened. This annoyed me, as I would, now, be forced to *prepare* to die again, which is not easy. It is a kind of shutting of the eyes and brain while smiling, which is not normal behaviour, and requires concentrated effort. I lay tidily in preparation.

Suddenly, someone said, for my eyes were shut, that what had happened when I had thought that nothing had happened, was that she had injected me with something to make me drowsy, before the anaesthetic proper. This is, apparently, thought to be a small, helpful, and even desirable thing: but it was not. I had prepared for this moment for weeks. And now things were being done without warning. I would have felt wounded by thoughtlessness, had not my feelings been drowsed, which is a nice conundrum, and rather neat. I resigned myself to the fact that I was not now going to be told when the Small Death was coming, which very soon I might not care about anyway, or whose message I might not now bother to understand, and so was forced to assume a ridiculous Condemned position and expression, while keeping my eyes closed, and making sure I was vaguely aware enough to see the drama of extinction, no matter in what careless dress it might now appear, coming.

On the whole, the effort was worth it, I think. The whole thing was *delicious*. There was no spirit-level struggle: obliteration arrived in the form of an amusing lemon sherbet DibDab wing of an Angel, which I saw completely coming, and knew was Nice. It lifted me into the light. I have thought since that if Death is like this, then it is not so bad. But of course that would only be the *moment* of death. The following eternity of nothing does not have much to recommend it.

What happened in the hour following has been told to me since.

A tiny incision was made in my navel, or in *the* navel, as I had by then given up any real attempt to be Me, the parts that understood that phenomenon having been drugged unto darkness. Ah, but it was not Intelligence or Creation, then, that needed its number sleep, but that part of the brain that protested, usually, at the damage of the Body. A tube was then inserted into this hole, and *the body*, unapprehended by My Self or by Its Self, filled with some gas, in order to create a kind of marquee in which there was room to run about and perform the Operation more breezily. Two more tiny incisions were made in the left and right sides, one for a camera and the other for Putting Things In. A long piece of Gortex (I am not sure if this bit is right, but then I was not there, in one sense, after all, to check, and there is no chance of finding out now) was stapled across the sewn-up muscle, to keep everything in place forever. How a piece of anything managed to get in via the Tiny Holes is beyond me. People have muttered since about umbrellas, and ships in bottles, but I am none the wiser. And after an hour of slicing, blood, staples and care, it was done.

I like to think, I am not sure why, that the whole thing took only a minute or two, and was done by magic, because the admission that I, that is, my body, and with it all my creative and intelligent thoughts, the plans for my sonnets I had not written down yet, the physical and mental details of the characters I was creating in 'Molecule', my ready rhymes and mental thesaurus, the immeasurable complex of thoughts and memories I use to create, left life-as-it-is-known for an hour and more, during which things were done to me that I could not have borne had I the merest squiddle of consciousness, alters my perception entirely of what it is to Live and Be, and of what I am. I was breathed for (because the pneumatic marquee pressed so hard on the diaphragm that it could not function: this is normal and planned), and unconscious, but still, somehow, Me. For that long, but imaginably short, hour, then, not only did I lose control, and my Self, but, as well, my dominating Machine, the perfect product of so many millions of years of refinement for survival, was kept going by some Men, with some Machines of their own.

Which implies an almost abstract conspiracy of persistence: which, in turn, implies, nay advertises, that there is, and I am, Something Worth Being. This is really *Something Else*.

I do not understand the eloquence of my body. Now that it is back, miraculously breathing and beating without the slightest intent or effort on my (whichever Me the My comes from) part, I am more determined than ever to discover what Evolution has made me, and to connect somehow with the blind, pushy, selfish, unbelievably complex and surprisingly thinking thing that had begun my Operation by kindly dulling my wish to thought. For I am in love with it. By comparison, the twiddlings of my creative spirit seem like silly sugar decorations on a cake. Maybe it is possible to find Creation in what has been done for me, and not by me: maybe what I am should be less my twitterings, than my manliness.

I awoke in a Waking Up Room, holding hands with a nurse who informed me I was the smilingest person she had ever seen wake up in the Waking Up Room. I was surprised. How happy could a person *not* be upon discovering they were alive and mended after Death and Destruction? I was wheeled back to the ward grinning.

And as I recovered, re-entering the light and comfortable little world I so desperately needed then, the lingering presence of the blow-up gas affected me. I experienced agonising small pains like little poisoned bombs going off in my shoulders: I was *acutely retentive* (it said on the Complications Sheet): but, best of all, I was tail-endedly, and hauntingly, drugged.

I was moved to Isolation to sleep overnight. In this spooky, empty room, with a pair of shining, insectular taps, a television screen on a stick, and a plastic, flowered modesty-curtain that burbled in the breeze of passing wheelchairs, I dreamed wonderful, surrealistic dreams: a great, high, wide, skirted tree whose leaves were made of pumice stones: a gigantic porcupine bobbing on its back legs, weeping from a long, pale human face: then a thousand identical cyclists pedalling and nodding across a frozen lake: then a lobster before a pink curtain: and then a block of flats made from slices of toast. I wrote it all down, you may be sure.

For these were wonderful. The fear and alienation associated with them only made them more precious. The Isolation Room nurse told me that certain patients used to 'taking substances' had told her that these visions were of the highest order. And, indeed, they were. I asked her how they had described these Ecstasies: she said they said that they were 'surrealistic', 'like Dali'.

This was a creative bombshell.

A drug; a nameable, analysable drug, whose every element is known, is capable of manufacturing distinctive, creative pictures in human beings. Astonishingly, they are the same kind of pictures in everyone: that is, what is generally known as 'surreal'. No one, no matter how comprehensively learned, or careless, it appears, has ever had a 'Metaphysical', 'Georgian', 'Pastoral', 'Impressionistic', 'Romantic' or 'Post-Beckettian' dream, under these circumstances. This implies, nay, *means*, that the particular vision of Dali and the surrealists was a matter of pre-propensitising and urgent chemicals: whatever incited them to create and conceive what they did was some natural, or unnatural, brain-dosage of something from the molecular content of the gas that had been used to make me into a tent, in them, by administration, or, more amazingly still, not: that is, from some form of natural occurrence. It may be, then, that we are born little Tennysonians and little Spenserians. We all know, after all, that each of us has things that we '*naturally*' and unaccountably like, respond to and prefer in life, be they countries, food, writers, film stars, music, sports, or colours, and this, I now appreciated, is a prefabricated chemical reaction: which is why it is unaccountable. It does not belong to our silly little minds: it belongs to that buried, wonderful part of us that I have called Evolution. Life's experiences are the twinkly bibbles on a biscuit; but it is these chemicals, these gifts of Evolution, or that unknown part of us that I am determined to discover, that give us our real Life in its most creative, passionate and committed forms.

Now I am home, and writing 'Molecule' again. What will it be? For how can I live now with a part of me that is vital, huge, active, kind, age-old, impossibly complex, quiet, self-preserving, scientifically urgent and fabulously creative, and not try to know it? Once when I was attacked by dogs in Turkey, this part of me prepared me to die by shooting me full of pain- and terror-dulling chemicals. What Evolution that was. But it was also Me. And I will find it. Because it is *here*.

Ah, imagine then, writing with that complete person: some thing with the practice of millions of years, with refinements and urges that we glimpse only occasionally, and if we are lucky: maybe three or four times in our lives. Our lives. Not just the pretty poems, the petty feelings and thoughts we have about people and things, relationships and rivers, the safe dangers, the childhood senses, travels and craven images, but the ones about how a cut mends, how our hearts beat, and how on earth something so great as we are is made for us to be for such a short time, and what a terrible opportunity is there.

> Yet all these were when no man did them know,
> Yet haue from wisest ages hidden beene
> And later times thinges more vnknowne shall show.

As for *The Faerie Queene*, I am galloping past Canto 4, looking for that Best Adventure, and dragging with me my beautiful burden of life.

The Story of Molecule

1 Molecule leaves home

And then he wrote um *fuck of Evolushin* –
and nearly then *bcoz,* but not *bcoz*
because the rolly-paper was too small.
fuck of evolushin dash was all
he wrote, and that was it: and so it was
that Molecule began his Revolution,
puffed the paper, chucked the pen away,
considered all his twelve interminable,
automatic years, walked out the door
and left Mankind. The moon was blue. No more
the fatal heart, the uncontrollabibble
urge, the hunted soul, the driven day.

The drive went *crick* and *crack*, and he was gone.
The world was all asleep. The soft stars shone.

2   *he goes back for his bike*

He stopped. His upright, bright-brown shadow splashed
along the verge like some advertisement
for Progress. Crap. He went back for his bike.
The shed was locked. Some clouds assembled, gag-like,
round the moon. His Raleigh Record Sprint.
His Betterer of Beasts. He bished and bashed
the door down *sssh* and stickly rode away,
a complicated, undictated shape
made up of Molecule, machine, and night.
The little shops of Richmond slept. One pinlight
pricked the walls at FreshPak. And an ape
on bits of metal jiggled by. And day,

impatient, urgent, flushed and bursting, leaked
across the fading, baffled moon, and peeked.

3   Dad wakes up

Coff–coff–coff. What now. What else. What for.
Another bloody day. Ah – Work. Because …?
Ah – Molecule: they willy-nilled each other.
Better neither really. And his mother.
Um what would a Man do then? What was
the point of freedom? Coff–coff– yaaaawn. What more
was there than being born, then kids, then Shove-Off
eh? That's why we're here. So smoke and shave,
a note – *B gd @ skool c u @ 6 –*
the old, reluctant car, the josh, the bricks,
the day by day, the kids leave home, the brave
and busy lie, the bloody waste coff–coff –

O jeez who cares? One empty bed said *me.*
One pittered drive. One bashed-up shed. One free.

4 Molecule spends the day asleep

Day was disappointed. Molecule
pedadalled rudely into Isel Park
and slept beneath the conifers while all
the Other World dumb-danced its busy ball.
He woke up when the sky went gluely dark
and jiggled on: and this nocturnal school
taught only Nothing, Emptiness and Peace.
What had he missed, asleep amongst the warm,
browncrackled twiglets? Just some Soulsdeath Dance:
old habit's steps, the stamping-down of chance,
the whirling gowns of doodledom, the swarm
of Evolution, grinning, strict, obese.

Tahuna Beach. He got off. Bubbly foam
moved the unmoved sand. Which felt like home.

5   *Tahuna Beach*

He plonked down in the sparsey dunes. The sea's
delicious lead-sheet gleamed. He put his head
all snugger on the saddle. Stars like glass:
baleful seagulls: toiling marramgrass.
All blind to Man. He might as well be dead.
Perfect. Molecule sat up. The pinetrees
floffed. Two girls with buggies pushed along
the moonwet sandflats, moonlight-armoured, singing
to their babies. Kittens have evolved
their cuteness to Survive: and wheat has solved
its clueless biogenesis by springing
Bread-for-Man-ly from the earth. The song

blew sweet away. And more live to make more.
The ocean dutifully swept the shore.

6   *Mr Gillies goes to the police*

Mr Gillies stared. The crackered shed.
The truant bike. He searched the house. A haze
of brickdust rosed his shirt. No Molecule.
He texted Auntie Jack. He phoned the school.
Fucking Nora: *absent eighteen days.*
He rang the police in coral puffs. They said
they'd find him Tootdersweet. They said a kid
just wants its famlee. Mr Gillies tried
describing Molecule, but couldn't. Well,
they said, just find a photo. Who can tell
what children want? He couldn't. Then he cried.
They said Come down to Queen Street. So he did.

His son sat grinning blankly at the sea.
Can a boy be Missing who is Free?

7   *Molecule reaches Nelson Cathedral*

Next night the bike was seen near Anzac Park –
but only by a pigeon up a pine.
Humanity lay busily in bed,
its batteries recharging. And they said,
We'll get him back. But Molecule was fine.
He wobbled up Trafalgar Street. The dark
cathedral tower said, Sweetheart! Ride to me!
He did. For man was never made to love
some bloody God unless he made Him. More
than Mum and Dad. He looked up. And ignore
the Bastard Evolution. Good. Above,
the pigeon burbled up a Christmas tree.

And by the time God got there he was gone.
The police as well. He smiled and pedalled on.

8 *dawn at Atawhai*

The tide was out. Fat valvous things blew bubholes
in the mud. He dropped his bike. And in
the empty Waiting Room of dawn he listened
to their cries. The dutied sunshine glistened
on their doomlives like a burning skin.
They blubbled, squeaked and twittered: and their souls
despaired. He blundered in to free them – dead,
blind-buried, poor perpetuating slaves
of Evolution. Crap. He sat down *splot*.
Miles of wakened, burbling, clockwork, lifehot
mud. Like people living in their graves.
His hands dried crisp. His nails went black and bled.

He slept the purblind sleep of worms and dreamed
of weeds. The tide slid in. The seagulls screamed.

9 Dad and Auntie Jack talk

Under the spreading Christmas tree-thing Dad
and Auntie Jack had one more beer and wondered
what the jeezis Molecule was up to.
Baubles stabbed their heads with lightpins. Zap-blue
tinsel bristled. Angel-glints rotundaed
round the horsewallpaper. 'Zlookin bad,'
said Dad. He snorted. 'Jeff he's probly sitting
up at Nana's' – 'Been there' – 'down some friend's eh?' –
'Phoned em all' – 'or up Poutama Street
with bloody Wig and Steff.' The noontide heat
like lard. Dad drooped. Day 3. 'Jeff you OK?'
The house creaked. Aunty Jack resumed her knitting.

Daylight dazzlefied the Christmas balls.
Electric Angels unctioned round the walls.

10   Molecule is seen near Cable Bay

Canopus twinkled, cold and hopeless-far.
What use is names? Wakapuaka. Comfort-
badges. Wakapuaka. Moonlight waxed like
Golden Syrup. Creak, creakcreak, the bike
bumped down to Cable Bay. Beef-bound dumb-shit
cows looked out with big glass eyes. A car
shone past the other way. And stopped. Drove on.
And stopped. The bush, the streets, the stars, and me,
all named for Man's illusion of control.
Drove on. He dug himself a pebble-hole
and watched the tireless silver-shiny sea
dance round all night. And all the dead stars shone.

And stopped. White moonlight snuffled round the car.
Hello? A child. Just now. Near Maori Pa.

11   *nearly nearly near Hira*

The police car gasped and bobbled. *Thass a bush.*
It burbled on to Cable Bay. Just then,
Molecule emerged, his piss complete.
They torchy-searched the beach. Their stumble-feet
all clonked and wet. They drove around the Glen.
The sun leaked up. He went unconscious. Shush.
They doubled back, then forth, then round again,
then drove right past him, bag-wrapped, safe and sound
asleep behind a dump of fenceposts. Good.
The stars dance thus: but with some understood,
coldclear design – while Man's hot lost-and-found
all fails and falls, conjunctionless and vain.

The schoolkids went to school. The clouds bobbed by.
The police went home. The poplars kissed the sky.

12 Molecule gets blown over

Next night he elbowed up the Whangamoa.
A locust on a pair of glasses. Blam!
Thudder! Whoosh! A logging truck came banging
down the bend, its two great eyelights hanging
in the dust. He wobbled. BOOOOP! Wham!
The weightwind boffed him over. BOOOOP! The blower
booped again – its serried bumlight shone
away like sparkly sweets into a gob.
Crap. His bikewheel whizzed. The stars advised
a stoic rally: Molecule, capsized
amidst a careless sea, complied. A blob
of blood rosed through his shirt. He got back on.

Huge land. Huge night. Huge time. Huge world. A child.
A bike. A road. And nothing owed. He smiled.

13 *his dream on Whangamoa Saddle*

Consider trees. They neither think nor walk.
But God or Something clothes them, green and green,
denudes them, roots them, photosynthesises,
keeps aloft, rebuds and multiplises,
blahblah blahblah blahblah all the unseen
rude mechanics stuck in every stalk
and twiglet, leaf and stock and needle for
the self-perpetuating-serving round
of sad survival. Jeez. So many trees.
So busy-blind. A gentle midday breeze
ruffled them for miles. The flibbling sound
deeped in his sleep. The forest worked. What more

is Man? His More is Knowing This Is So.
What makes him man? To move. To think. To know.

14 *Molecule spreads the word*

He woke. The sun escaped behind the hills.
An now, he told the trees, I'm goin to say
evrything I know an stay awake
until I dun. And through the gentle ache
of night, when Certainty unfinds its way,
and Man feels most alone, when rumpus fills
the brightest hearts, he publicised his brain
across the managed, whispering valley while
the moonlight painted it – phone numbers, faces,
songwords, swearwords, cars, addresses, places …
soft above the rooted bush his fragile
knowledge rippled like an aeroplane.

The pilot slept. A truck banged by. He dreamed
of sunrise like a raygun. Birdies screamed.

15 Mr Gillies wraps his Christmas presents

Richmond. Cheyne Walk. Sunday. Cats and dogs
yawned on lawns. Clean cars. Hot lunches. Beer.
The sick, unquestioned, valuable day.
Remains of some beheld religion lay
like lead across men's souls, and work, like fear,
infected what it followed. Monologues
of distant radios. A mower-hum.
Auntie Jack; the mean departed wife;
Molecule; and Nana. That was it.
Four presents lumped in santawrap. Aw shit.
Four biologic loves. Is that my life?
Four pairs of socks. Is that what dreams become?

O Molecule! He watched TV and wept.
How freedom hurts. Do do, then die. He slept.

16   Molecule eats at the Something Oven

Midnight. Molecule rolled in to Rai.
His stomach *gurgled*. How come Evolution
can't make Air our Food if it's so bloody
clever? Shovel, chew and shit. A muddy
bibble out of someone's hose: a bin
behind the Something Oven. *Burp*. A fly,
all stitched with starlight, watched this little town
so shortly won from Greenness, satisfy,
unconscious and uncalled, a Fellow Man.
And if we make compulsions art we can
believe we have a Soul. The twinkling sky
shone out like something Good. The moon smiled down.

The bush-surrounded Something Oven shone,
misgiven in its night. He pedalled on.

17 *Molecule is confirmed alive by a day-person*

He reached Pelorus Bridge and slept beside
the river in a nest of round warm stones,
his little head unsorry on the saddle.
At midday someone came down for a paddle.
Pie-and-Pepsi-balanced, Witi Jones
was bibbling in the shallows when he spied
a body. Whoa! He splosh-clacked closer. It
was working. Like a bunch of bones begotten
by the sun. That afternoon, in Rai,
this vision lighted on his inner eye
and made him smile: that Someone had forgotten
how to live what he was living. Shit.

He fitted half a shower, tiled and grouted
half a bathroom, drove back home – and doubted.

18   Molecule goes for a swim

Molecule woke up at dusk. The river
silver-swirled a pool here just below
the bridge. A ruru hooed. He waded in.
The pebbles rolled his feet. His milky skin
prickled in the cool. The to-and-fro
of easy-going currents made him shiver.
He lay back in the water's bounce-and-glow.
Above, great totara-crowns turned in the sky
with silhouettes of settling birds. A truck
threw yellow through the bridge-struts. Glooping, moonstruck
trout nibbled round his knees. A bushfly
glittered. Stars streamed in the undertow.

No Man dares to call this Life: so no one
came. He swam. They waited for the sun.

19   *he visits the giant totara*

He stood before the ancient tree. He searched
its face for Wisdom, Patience, Love, Denial,
Courage, Purity, Experience,
for something Mighty, Honour in a Prince
of Age, some natural Awe, some Wizard-smile.
But all he saw was blank constraint. It lurched
at Heaven agely rooted to its grave.
It human-seemed, with arms and trunk and hair,
but blankly waved its leaves and sucked its food
in brainless, dutied, thankless solitude.
And yet how Mighty! Strangers to despair,
the trees kept Living, vacuously brave.

Molecule stepped up and kissed its bark.
Good on yer, eh. It laboured in the dark.

DS Baigent stretched his sandals. *Right.*
One-six-three-two ... missing 1st December ...
4 Cheyne Walk um Richmond ... name: Molloy
Gillies ... ('Molecule') (?) – (please check this) – boy ...
12 ... hair: light ... shoes/clothes: er can't remember ...
skinny short (need details??) ... Catholic (???) ... white ...
list of family ... list of friends ... one sighting,
Cable Bay ... N. Randall (68),
4th December (time????) ... phone blahblahblah ...
Raleigh Record Sprint ... one car so far ...
print ... alert ... patrol ... re-search ... update ...
Right! He had a Twix. He started writing.

Queen Street buzzed with business. Sun poured through
its shops, and everyone knew What To Do.

Canvastown. He ditched his bike. The Trout.
He tiptoed past the golden windows. There,
provoked by urgent, human lights like suns,
some humans buzzed about. Their rods and guns
gleamed bright against the bar. The egging glare
of everything. They chattered. Stomped about.
Prepared. A car flashed past. A wakeyhead
came out to smoke her ciggie in the face
of darkness. Molecule bobbed down. And out
they marched! All torched and armed to battle trout
and deer, to claim the bolshie night and chase
all-anything that hadn't gone to bed.

He watched them go. The whooping carlights died
along Tapps Road. The vanished poplars sighed.

The Policing Centre walls, behung with snow,
wobbled in the heat. A plastic tree,
decked darkblueish, shimmered in a corner.
Scuttled whisperings of urban fauna,
servants of the sun and destiny,
bibbled in the bogus mistletoe
and tickled through the tinsel. Man and Fly,
both plied their sunny, automatic trade,
their profit being Life. Maybe, somewhere,
some existential Ant who Didn't Care
lounged upon a glittered bauble, Stayed
Away, observed his friends, and Wondered Why.

Most likely not. For only Man can choose
to slight the Plan, to know it and refuse.

The last light dipped like sinking ships. He stuck
his fingers in a crackled log. And quick-night
ran down Highway 6. The river bibbled.
Yaaawn. Wee shiny glob-wet grublets nibbled
in his palm. He watched them wiggle, white
with strange intent. And then he ate them, guck
and crunch. He crawled across the rattle-bank
and lapped his breakfast while the bright moon rolled
from A to B. The bush went black. Some blood
swirled off his underwater hand, and blue mud
twinkled at the splinters. Flecks of gold
fled like sudden sighs of love, and sank.

He watched while Evolution stitched his skin.
He poked the crackled splinters further in.

Of course she worried. Milo by the bed.
Everything locked up. The TV on.
She pulled the blankets back. Another day
defeated. Poor wee Molecule. She lay
luxuriously out. The bedlight shone
its cosy pool across the room. Her head
sank softly in familiar pillows. Silly ...
boy. The happy smells. The small content.
Everything you are in one safe place.
She yawned and smiled. Scratched from the Human Race
she nodded stilly in her element
and dreamed her dreams of friends and family.

The Milo skinned. Moths danced round the light.
And worry wasted on the summer night.

25   *how things are*

Molecule creaked into Havelock.
The ink sea swam. The stars all chatted light.
The National Police Computer System blipped
his Details. Yachts rubbed noses. Hawsers dripped.
Mussels muttered in their benthic night.
His finger festered. DS Baigent's clock
flipped off one more minute of our lives.
Dad and Nana, drugged with darkness, slept
their one glad hour. Possums picked the bush.
The whisper-fraying clouds. The glowy whoosh
of waves on jetty-legs. Taumaka crept
in shallow stones. Cars waited in their drives.

Nocturnal-pale and blank, he walked through town.
The windows filmed him pass. The moon looked down.

26 *no publicity please*

'Of course Sir, it's your choice.' The DS tapped
his Twix-to-come. 'But usually we find
with Missing Persons some Publicity
can help.' He leaned a little back. 'You see
er basic-lee the public are – um – *kind*.'
He leaned a little further back. 'They're apt
to – um – respect – er, decent, normal things
like famlees, friends and ... that' (his huka voice).
But somehow Mr Gillies knew his son
wanted to be Missed: to be someone
not Lost but Gone. 'Of course Sir, it's your choice.
Like I said.' The angel blinked its wings.

And Dad went back to work. He laid his bricks
like love, while DS Baigent ate his Twix.

And while he worked he thought of all the things
that seemed to make his son unhappy. One
per brick. Like food, relations, sleeping, bullshit,
Christmas, birthdays, TV, talking, schoolshit,
kittens, houses blah blah blah. The sun
smiled sweetly on his wall. Whatever brings
that whole Belonging Thing was missing ... Yet
he knew that happiness was possible.
Perhaps that's what he'd run away to do:
to find it Elsewhere. Like his mother. Who
had once said, 'Jeff, we're in a prison full
of crap.' The sun worked hard. The mortar set.

He went to Auntie Jack's. They had a beer
outside. The sky was comfortless and clear.

28   *sex on a windy road*

He took the windy road to Moenui.
He pushed his bike up every little hill.
The wide world whispered. Wonder-warm and vast,
the sense of sea slipped round him as he passed.
And then he rattled down. The houses, still
and lightless, fortified their Men. A tui
creaked amongst the bushtops. Then *a car* –
halfshut, halflit, parked up beneath the hang
of glossy leaves. He stopped. Picked up his bike
and tiptoed past. Inside, a white bum like
a fish gasped at the moon. A muffled bang-
abang-abang, a gentle ah–ah–ah.

While Evolution thrived, he sat apart
and watched the sea, and listened to his heart.

Gidday I'm You. You started when I did.
You'll finish when I do. The rest is bubbles,
baubles, bric-a-brac and booby-breath.
Ker-thump. I am your Engine Unto Death.
And you are just a juggernaut of troubles,
pain, ambition, vanity, assorted
bosh and bollocks roaring down Completely
Artificial Purpose Avenue.
Ker-thump. And Driving Unto Death. My love,
there is no point to us, no God above,
no art, no power, no nothing right or true,
but just this dull red thud of you and me.

The moon slipped down. He snuggled round his bike.
And thought: *but I kin stop us when I like.*

He woke up in the middle of the day
all lapped in ferns. The sparkling bite of blue
wrinkled hot and happy. Tall yachts rolled
like smiling metronomes. The sky was gold.
He rubbed his eyes and yawned. A pair of kahu
driftly inked in 'o's above the bay.
And higher up – another bird! It sheered,
and chattered like a zip, and scissored bright
across their soar. He sprinted. Bushtops banged like
shutters over every move. His bike!
He scrabbled up. He dragged it out of sight.
Two police cars. Prowled. Spied by. And disappeared.

He half went back to sleep. His finger throbbed.
The police cars somewhere else. The white yachts bobbed.

31   *how he was*

Half-asleep in sunshine. Sticky hair
(but still a fuzz) nestling in the bushmould.
Sort of yellow skull. Grub-tongue. Fur-teeth.
Wee black shirt with flames on. Underneath
two boatprow ribends. Septic finger. Big-old
army pants. With oily rips. A pair
of too-big bargain trainers. Just five stone
of human being being by his bike.
A tiny neck-pulse. Twitches. Bleeding shin.
Ratty. Flapears. Bitnails. Scabby. Thin.
Runny nose. Big smile-teeth. Bobbing birdlike
breath. And now and then a rustly moan.

His metal mount lay next to him without
the burden of a life; its faith, its doubt.

Three hundred corners later. Ten to ten.
He watched the floating ferry-weddingcake
crown out into the Sounds. He yawned. His wee
nocturnal being drooped and dropped. A bee
like some Advertisement for Being Awake
busied round his sticky eyes: and when
the Arahura burbled in that night,
its decks aswarm with sunny souls, he woke
and squashed it with his trainer. People whooped
and waved. The sun went ginger. Seagulls swooped
around the wakespray. Man Has Conquered. Smoke,
belief and engines. Silence raped with light.

The foreshore filled with children. Darkness fed
their brief rebellion. 'Join us,' someone said.

33   *on the foreshore*

They sat amongst the garbage of success,
dignified by ugliness and waste,
indifferent to the self-preserving laws
of Men and Nature, careless of the cause
of order, quiet, strange and wayward-faced.
Molecule sat down. They tried to guess,
but did not ask, why he was there. They played,
they drank, they talked, they smoked, they phoned, they smiled,
they dreamed, they gave him this and that, but mostly
they were quiet. Moonlight pearled a ghostly
sheen across the town and sea. Beguiled
by light and misfit company, he stayed.

We gotta go. They drifted off. And sorrow
vanished with them. Pity their Tomorrow.

34   *elevation and balance*

He squedalled out of town. A stain of light
seeped out along the sky-skirts. One car came.
Halfway up the Elevation culvert
Molecule fell off. His finger hurt.
His brain went *bloop*. A little tarry flame
licked out his Fact. A sort of mental night
followed on the natural one. *Now I'm
a stone*, he thought (except he didn't think).
And what was *that*? His metal mathsy-bike
presented all its angles, vector-like,
amongst the air. He smiled. The sky turned pink.
Nothing to be done. There wasn't Time.

And then it dwindled. Evolution healed
our hero. Crap. He slept in someone's field.

Something woke him. Tyres and gravel. Two
doors slammed. Bangbang. He sat up. Crap again.
Ten yards away. A black Toyota van.
Two people. Shouts. Nowhere to hide. The man
yelled. She yelled. They waved their arms. And then
she got back in. The sky glared fierce and blue.
The sun grilled sandflies on the paintwork. Sheep
ripped up the grass. The stretch-hot fencewires squealed.
He got back in. Brmbrm. They roared away.
The busy, burning, angry day. He lay
back down. The roadtar popped and blobbed. The field
staled its smell. He fluttered back to sleep.

And where the tyres had shuddered was a blot
of blood. Too bright. Too close. Too cruel. Too hot.

36 Jeff visits Wig and Steff

Two yellow Buell XD-onetwoRs
leaned like resting kings against the fence
at number 24 Poutama Street.
Inside they talked, all beery-spliffered. Heat
ironed the kitchen floor. 'It doan make sense,'
said Wig. They mooned in smoke. Piwakawakas
squibbled in the garden toitois. 'Hey –'
Steff took Jeff's hand and smiled – 'Just leave him be.
Eh?' – 'I reckon.' – 'Yep.' He spun his beer.
The sun bloomed in it. 'People disappear.
Maybe they just have genes that set them free.'
'You mean we aren't?' 'Dunno. *He'll be OK.*'

He drove back home. A little misfit sorrow
brushed his heart and vanished. Work tomorrow.

37 *Jesus lights in Blenheim*

Disturbed, he started early. Light still licked –
though lower, lower, lower – round the rim
of physic sky. His pus-blown finger throbbed
the tapey handlebar. His wee skull bobbed.
His black shirt flamed. He bowled on into Blenheim.
Him and High Street. Christmas shot-lights pricked
the dark. A dazzled progress: Jesus – Mankind –
Freedom. Coloured sparkles, strobes and dives.
But in this storm of Love and Life Men tie
themselves to other men with tinsel. High
above the white stars winked their longlost lives
away again, electric-clockwork-blind.

And God's great Overturning shall be read
from books of fierce convention by the Dead.

Blenheim floated in eternity,
a little lit. We know we are alone,
and huddle to our kind for sweet distraction
from that horror, feigning satisfaction
in some mummery. And God, our own,
our best invention, will not make us free
as long as we neglect to claim His birth
for our own brains, and that the world's creation,
which we cede to Him, which thankfulness
precludes rebellion, is the synthesis
of our own fear of Nature, Separation
and unundrstanding of the Earth.

He wobbled into darkness. Dark trees chained
with lights thrashed on behind him. Then it rained.

39 *Molecule is sighted sleeping in a vineyard tractor*

Sun and drizzle. Shimmered dampness. Miles
of flatflap smirry grapes and bright-wire hiss.
Brmbrm. Screech. A camper full of Curries
(Mum and Dad, three kids, one dog, no worries)
pulled up on the roadside for a piss.
Dad and Russell stared across the piles
of waiting woodstakes. 'Hey Dad – look!' A leafpluck
tractor dressed in yellow tubes and braces
gleamed in one wet aisle. A sleeping, gold-lit,
rain-warped shape sat in the cab. 'Oh Shit.'
'Doan swear.' 'He's ded.' They stared. Still still. Their faces
glistened. 'Awesome.' 'C'mon Russell.' 'Fuck.'

And who reports what can't be true? The sky
all cleared and burned. The grapeground blotted dry.

40   *his chain comes off*

Seddon slept. Its twenty streets a fact
beneath the moon. He pumpled palely through.
His legs like puppet-dowels. His finger bled
a kind of glassy pus. A police car sped
through Dashwood, nosing north. A lonely kahu
lassoed stars. Ker-*lonk*! The bike-chain cracked
and jangled off. He stopped. And suddenly
a life-wide weariness unmoved him. Good.
He sat down on the road. With busy grubs
like dark commuters. TipTop wrappers. Smokestubs.
Bits of glass. Obedient garbage. Who could
fight five million years of Destiny?

Some did. Some do. Some will. He fixed his chain
and pumpled on. The sun winched up again.

41   Molecule's dream

He slept by Grassmere Pond. The water, thick
with sludged and crackled saltshine, glitter-skinned,
shone like Heaven's banner dipped in sin.
He dreamed of giants wading hills, their skin
as blue as sailors' shirts, their arms like wind,
their feet like wakas. Then they drowned. A slick
of liquid paua brimmed their stridden ground.
They fell as trees. Beneath the diamond calm
he saw their glued eyes flick. He woke up, sweat
ashining on his skin. His shirt was wet.
He snorted like a drowning man. One arm
was empty as a breeze. He turned around.

His eyes blinked in the glare. Two giants lay
asleep beside his bike. He crawled away.

42   Jeff Gillies sends a deceptive e-mail

Hello DS Baigent! How r you.
Thank you very much for looking for
my son. I know where he is eh. So
evrything is sorted now. I know
that he is with his mum. They r in Gore.
(Whangerei). *To prove that this is true*
I attatatch a photo where they are
together. Thank you for your help. Goodbye!
The router blinked. He had a shower, a beer,
and cheese on toast. A little laugh of fear
convulsed his brain. His thin electric lie
had freed him into danger. Ha ha ha.

He sat outside. The sky went red. Then black.
He thought he knew he wasn't coming back.

43   a fast ride to Ward

He never biked so fast. The giants strode
behind him, pulling nighttime like a flooded
lake of ether at his back. The chain
squealed. The tyres spat. A whiteface crane,
like some dark giants' familiar, gawed and scudded
on his head. Stoats stood in the road.
Ah lights at last! A flicker-fest of reindeer,
santas, sleighs and stars. An elf-thing beamed
'8 DAYS 2 XMAS', stuck in bulbs of snow.
He stopped. Spangled in the strobey glow
he shut his eyes. A curtain twitched. He dreamed
of manless, thoughtless darkness, calm and clear.

'yes … with a bike … a child … not sure … alright …
Ward Street … okay ….' A front room sewn with light.

DS Baigent ponderised his screen.
His Twix amelt. His sandals unfootfilled.
Molecule and Mum. The bright attachment.
Smiling-safe. I think not. Save and Print.
'Get Jeff Gillies down here.' Chocolate spilled
across the sunhot desk. The fax machine
squealed a weft. The printer too. The phone
played Mozart40. Gore, my arse. They smiled
their ancient smile of Happy Families. Why
would any decent father crucify
his hope in life, his testament, his child?
The chocolate dripped. No man is born alone.

For we are loved until we love. Queen Street
bled and burned. He hurried through the heat.

45   *Christmas thoughts at Atawhai*

Witi Jones stared out across the shallow
mudflats from his deck. Behind him gaped
his front room, decked in blowzy baubles blinking
in the sun: before him, blankly thinking
Otherwise, the manless world escaped
his heart. He smoked his smoke. Above the yellow
edge-of-earth the sun toiled up into
the clarity of nothing, like a man
departing cowardice for chivalry.
Bugger. 8 o'clock. He gulped his tea.
Showers to fit. Money to earn. His van
gleamed off. To spend on. Shit. The bay turned blue.

Half-in, half-out, a deck is just the spot
to make a Life Decision on – or not.

Bang! He got a puncture. Crap. He walked
to Mirza. Darkling grasshiss. Starlight twinkled
in his fuzz. The flattie squealed and flopped.
Peace spread like a gentle bomb. He stopped
to contemplate his finger. Dirty. Wrinkled.
Sore. But mended. Ssh! Some night-thing squawked
and flabbered out across the stars. A tink
of carlight thickened on his tooth-trimmed nail.
Two cars! – 4 headlamps! – Close! – And torches flashed
all round. Like gods in colanders they crashed
across a cattlestop – and stopped. The smug-pale
searchlight of the moon turned on him. *Plink!*

The cars exploded. Peace-possessed and still,
he watched them hurtling at him up the hill.

47 *what should Molecule do?*

Go baffled and bulleted down like Bonnie & Clyde?
Surrender with umble hadvantage like Jesus did?
Crow like Salome? Melt like Molloy? Or faint
like faeries? Burn and believe like any gold saint?
Get shot in the dark and be famous like Billy the Kid?
Die hornhold and hero-houtnumbered like Boromir died?
Jump off the Golden Gate Bridge? Stick a sword in his guts?
Cut his wrists in the bath while thinking of culture and beauty?
Set fire to himself? Eat poison? Drive into a wall?
Sink slowly all slashed and sublime like the Der-Dying Gaul?
Get blown up in some foreign field-thing while doing his duty?
Stand right on the railway line? Go fatally nuts?

He waited, all gawping and rabbit and bike while they sped
up towards him. The sun rose to watch. The horizon ran red.

'Molecule? You're goin home my lad.'
'Fuck off.' 'You alright son?' 'Gimme my bike.'
'Hey Andy – can we get this in the car?'
'I ain't movin mate.' 'Oh yes you are
Sonny Jim.' 'I ain't.' 'Let's go.' 'I doan like
cars they make me sick.' 'Get in.' 'You sad
fuck shit. I'm on me fucking holiday.'
'How about the roofrack?' 'Piss off.' 'Get –
in – the – car.' 'Fuck off.' 'Just cool it eh?'
'You gotta smoke?' 'GET IN THE CAR!' 'No way.'
'Hey Andy!' 'Fuckcuntshit.' 'Let's go.' 'Just – let –
me –.' 'Get the fuck off me.' 'Let's go.' 'You're gay.'

'Yep … we've gottim … yep … Cheyne Walk … will do.'
'Home for Christmas little man.' 'Fuck you.'

Home was home was home. 'You wanna beer?'
'No.' 'You wanna go to Nana's?' 'No.'
'You wanna – .' Crap. They sat and watched the lawn.
The sun inched through its sentence. Yawn yawn yawn.
Back an hour. That long? 'You wanna go
to Wig an Steff's?' 'Nono.' A hero's tear
abseiled down his private face. The kind
of tear that Christ and Bilbo Baggins shed;
the kind of tear that meant No Going Back,
No Home Serves after Glory. 'Aunty Jack
wants to see you, son.' He turned his head
away. A tahou called. 'I gotta find

the puncture stuff.' Whose silly world was this?
Whose house? Whose room? Whose stuff? Whose happiness?

'He's home.' 'Who's home?' 'Molloy.' The phone went beep.
Then beep again. Jeff heard her wander off.
'Mum?' The kettle clicked. *Two words (3,4):*
a weather forecast from Macbeth. The door
went phut. *Blue dish by Rimsky-Korsakov*
(5 letters). 'Edna?' Shit. She fell asleep,
past love, past duty ... 'Mum!?' ... and noddy-hot.
'We'll come and pick you up tomorrow yeah?'
Nothing. 'Don't forget your toothbrush eh.'
Dad hung up. A wife in Whangerei,
a son in shit, a mum in Metlifecare;
leavers, loners, loonies. Fuck the lot.

He wrote a note. He drove to Wakefield Quay.
He shucked his clothes and jumped into the sea.

Molecule spooled round the house. The moon
went with him, with an existential eye.
It was – not seemed – a painted box-thing tied
onto the earth, where people lived and died
in gene-yoked teams, though hardly knowing why;
a kind of unevicting, smowt cocoon
for things not wanting wings; decked out with stuff
to make their stay seem All There Is; because
they made it so. All alien-amazed
they swam from room to room together, gazed
on Hearth and Home, and wondered what it was.
The moon had none. The boy had had enough.

He took his bike and left. He never found
the note. But Mr Gillies hadn't drowned.

52   Mr Gillies' note and swim

Nor had he ever meant to. Thus the note:
I think u will b gone when I cum back.
O police this X. And I will tell the school
yr w yr mum. Plz ph me & b careful.
Dad. He swam to Boulder Bank. The black
water splashed with stars. A motorboat
fished silver with its moorline. Why did he
live like he did? So half-alive. So told.
By urges and by men. What was he? Cowed
with habit, dulled with duty, bent and bowed
by labour, fed content and pleasure, old
too young and crippled by conformity.

He sat down on the stranded stones. He saw
the deep cold truth. And splattered back to shore.

53   *same thing, different direction*

And Molecule proceeded nor' nor' west.
Appleby and Rabbit Island. Day
discovered boy and bike asleep among
the sand-dunes, smiling. All the world seemed young.
Lapped in towels of marram-grass, he lay
like something newly born and newly blessed.
Wavelets blibbed the rippled beach. The knobby
driftwood gleamed. Even the gaunt old pines
danced. Behind, the mountains loomed like proud
parents. Seagulls squawked. A single cloud
stood still above. The long and littered lines
of hightides wrote their careless poetry.

New beginnings want a pretty birth.
A noble nature. And a welcome earth.

DS Baigent shook the *Evening Mail*
(*Did He Jump?*) exact across his knees.
The dachshund snored. The world was neat and tidy.
Coffee. Chocolate. *Suicideediedee.*
Snap a Twix. Outside, his lemon trees
held forth their lemons. Roses rosied, pale
and heavy. Grass made grass. The evening sky
made evening. All was well. Except for Man.
How complicated–stupid could you get?
Acting like it mattered. Lurv I bet.
Or money. Sip. *A black Toyota van.*
Ah, life could be so comfy. Why oh why?

The ferry blinked away. The sea was cold.
He sank. And sunshine washed the water gold.

55　*another night at Rabbit Island*

He sat and watched the moon all night. His head
in superslowmo. Up … then down … . The tide
slid wisps and whispers at him, then retreated.
Thirty thousand heartbeats. Pines repeated
what the wind said. Sleepy seagulls cried
like fading instincts. Ssh. The Will is dead,
and Wisdom's tired knot unravelled. What
lived now lived without travail or thought.
Some say the Hermit knows himself. Some say
the mess we make of life is life. Some say
renounce. And some say fight. Some say we ought
to just get on with it. And some say Not.

Who cares. Dawn bleached the moon. The seaswish swept
the sand. His heart kept beating while he slept.

56   *Sunday the 21st of December*

Christmas Canter. Richmond Pony Club.
River Terrace Road for Lee Valley.
8 o'clock. Thermos/kidz a Must!
Aunty Jack bib-bobbed up Hill Street. Dust
lazied in her kidspace. Sturmer Sally
trotted dully. Clipclop ... gravel ... scrub ...
hot sun ... blue sky ... top-dressing planes ... the ping
of shifting fencewires ... bump-bent fields ... the far
parade of mountains ... horsesnorts ... saddlesqueaks ...
and tackle-clink ... she nodded ... bibbling creeks ...
We Three Kings clipclop of Orient Are ...
Good King Wenceslas Looked Out ... BINGBING!

'Jeff?' 'He's gone.' The horse looked round. Clipstop.
'Okay ... I will Jeff ... seeya ... bye.' ... Clipclop.

All stately-slow at midnight, Molecule
pedadalled past the ghosts of Seifried's grapes.
The Coastal Highway gleered ahead like honey.
'Let im go,' said Jeff. He smiled. 'It's funny …'
Jack kept knitting. 'What?' The ghosty shapes
of piupius spooled the deck. The yellow wool
jigged up towards her hands like fishing line.
He glided past the mudflats. *WHITEBAIT HERE.*
Their little gluey eyes. 'You'd think you'd know
your own son, Jack.' They smoked. A Welcome Swallow
flittered in the kowhai. 'Why?' More beer.
'Because he's me.' They drank. 'Because he's mine.'

PIPPINS HERE. Their little lightheads piled
in moonlit fellowship. And gone. He smiled.

The wharfplanks rattled plankly. Through the gaps
the lip-lap tide. The niff of muddy gloop
and ... mmm! The fish reeled in the man. A bin
of restaurant relics! Jeez. He gargoyled in.
A stinky slop of lovelies: mussels, sludge-soup,
chowder-chunder, garlic toasties, troutscraps,
coffee-groundlings, buttersplots, an After
Dinner Mint ... and deeper, darker things.
Every dish is shit: but delectation
mocks the need. He chawed his cold collation
sitting on the jetty-end while rings
of moonlight jibbled on the sea like laughter.

He dreamed of them. Unnecessary joy
unwed the world, and satisfied the boy.

He slept in someone's empty section, wrapped
in cutty-grass. And all day Christmas cars
brrrmed back and forth, contentedly intent
and glittering with gifts, each kindly meant
to make the giver safe: a sea of stars
and shiny paper. And the tide lap-lapped
the jetty piles, and glittered down. And then
the Metlifecare big-minibus rolled up.
And while her grandson sunslept in the grass
behind her, Edna Gillies bought a glass
raccoon, an Earendil Elfin cup,
a Drawer-Fresh, and an 'I Heart Jonah' pen.

'From Nana xxxx to Molloy
Bon Voyage my sweetheart darling Boy.'

Molecule unwrapped. The long grass sighed
and perked. He cranked down Aranui Road.
The moon was somewhere else. He passed a bach
whose bright, unblinded window splodged a patch
of houselight in his way. He swerved. He rode
a little past. He stopped. He stared. Inside,
a sofa stuffed with people staring back.
Nine. The TV lights reflected on
their faces. Drowning in their cushion-ships.
Each one held a pack of Murphy's chips –
entranced, agape, becalmed. Their big eyes shone
like foglamps still at sea. The rest was black.

Sourcream and chives. He scooted. Creaked away.
The moonless flatwaves rattled Ruby Bay.

61 Ruby Bay

He sat down on the stony beach. His bike
sat down beside him. Night and mud and tides.
And something – ssh! Crackpop. Click-clatter. Clack.
And Bounce. Goosebumps. Behind them, biscuit-black
and beetling-crumb the cliffs lost little slides
of their existence. Pitching pines stuck out like
snapped umbrellas, sifting needles, fust
and barkbits on the hangi-stones below.
They slowly turned to look. When Great Men Fall
we mostly smile, because we know that all
our busyness is death. When Great Things Go
To Pieces all our certainties are dust.

Which cheered them up. They watched the slow decay
of immortality – and rode away.

Next night he hit a flying *Nelson Mail*.
Its wings wrapped round his head. He fell off. Bang.
He bounced across the gravel. Smacksmacksmack.
The headlines justread: *Picton Ferry Black*
Toyota Mystery Man. And something rang
a bell. A little blot. A red detail.
Too bright. Too cruel. Too something. Blood bled through
one pantsknee. Shouting ... burning paint. He sat
and watched the paper soar like some soul-clapped
toroa past the moon. His bike brake snapped
all by itself. Ping-ping. He hoiked. He spat.
A blob of red. And something fiercely blue.

He crankered on. Scabs crisped across his knee.
He bombed unbraked down Motueka Quay.

63   Motueka

The clock tower gongled Christmas Bong Bong Eve.
He wheeled his bike down High Street. Posies, hot pies,
parkas, snowboards, jandals, diamond rings,
bananas, beer, paintrollers, fairies, things
as thronging as the stars. His slewy eyes
reflected all the floundered silver sleave
of eyeless fealty. He stayed awake.
He sat outside the glittered church and waited
for the sun. And while he watched, the world
became its families. He smiled. He curled
contented in the grass. The complicated
kin converged, and Christmas had its cake.

A giant chocolate Guardian Angel gleamed
and melted in a window. High Street beamed.

And then he slept the whole day through. Come night,
he upped and clattered on between the tents
and troops of hops and appletrees, that strung
their bated breaths beneath the moon, which hung
in Heaven like some God of Fruit, their scents
all heady-pleached. The tarmac sparkled, bright
and crackly as a saltrow. Christmas came
unnoticed to the world. He passed Kaiteri
Road. No Molecule of Molecule
evolved to know the day. He stopped. The hushful
dark possessed him. Good. He sat down. Merry
What. He smiled. The earth was all the same.

In hilly folds and valleys houses waited
for the Different Day they had created.

And this is God: that all around the thought
of Him runs busyness, and faith, and mind
enough to save us from the black machines
that we are made to be. Amongst our genes
lurks one miraculous desire to find
Our Saviour, which is Sillynesse – untaught,
unevolutionary Fibs With Art.
Of course we know that in the end we die,
and It removes us, having had the chance
to multiply: but what the fuck. So dance,
mankind, your hopeful dances, laugh and cry
as if it matters, dream you have a heart.

Oh Lord Our God, defend us, and forgive
the human lies we figure forth to live.

His opened eye before the moon's: the flap
of jandals: *swoosh!* The hop-hedge parted. 'Who
the hell are you?' He stood up sleepy. Quick.
A story. Think! He whined. 'I just been sick.
I got this bike for Christmas. It ain't new.
Daddy's on the dole. We got a van.' Oh crap.
He picked his nose. 'I'm goin to show my mum.
She lives in Motueka.' 'Go on son.'
The farmer's eyes were bright with tears. 'Take this.'
Ten dollars! 'Thank you sir.' 'And Happy Christmas.'
Off he wobbled. Waving. While the sun
went down in goldness. Back the way he'd come.

He waited by Kaiteri Road until
it darked. Then crankled back towards the Hill.

67   *on Takaka Hill*

The money crackled in his pants. He trudged
the zigzags steeply up and up, his bike
chit-chattering beside him. Dust like words.
Some faroff fireworks glittered. Tiptoe birds
clicked in fragile root-twists. Marble rucks like
ghosts in conference. Distant seashine smudged
with sleevey night-clouds. Up and up. And soon
he reached Hawkes Lookout. Trayed in lucent space
he watched the wrinkled world about its rote,
more lovely, empty, will-less and remote
than he. What beauty. Ah what peace. His face,
all white and thin, lent living to the moon.

Another rocket bubbled in the sky.
And then the pop. And then the falling sigh.

Three hours on he reached the top. The air
all luminous. One fond light blinkled on
the other side below. He waited for
his heart. He watched a great birdshadow soar
along the looping roadfall. Moonlight shone
in alabaster rounds; and everywhere
the quiet beat of life ran slow and still.
And far away, the Gillies slept, beer-battered,
bored, and turkey-stuffed, their socks unwrapped,
their souls unsatisfied. A bauble tapped
the TV. Left-cream staled. And cakecrumbs pattered
paper plates. He started down the hill.

They stirred and strained and whispered in their sleep.
Too wild. Too dangerous. Too fast. Too steep.

And down he flew! Yeee-haaaa! The tyres asqueal,
the wheel-propellers, trainer-laces snapping,
gulping pants, flickflacking shirtflames, ribs
clickclack like castanets, and little blibs
of snot like rubber-bands, his big ears flapping,
judder eyeballs jelly, glockenspiel
of teeth, skidskids, flingflings, swerveswerves, shockshocks,
bone-bouncing, headfuzz ripping air like matches
on a strike-strip, legs so fast they ran
on atoms, goggle tongueflap, BirdBoy, JetMan,
wheeeee! his cheeks like slap-sails, bug-detatchers,
button-whirrers, throaty-wobblers, frame-knocks,

chain-chocks, spit-suck, piping flute-mouth OOOOO
and EEEEE, and down, and down ... and down ... and ... phew.

70 *friends*

He slept against a deerfence. Through it, two
soft-questing nostrils hoovered in his hair.
He kicked his bike adream. The deer quick-clittered
off. The sun like glass. The fencewire glittered
razor-bright. He woke. A nibbling pair
of strut pukekos waffled in the dew.
His own sweet-sloven smell hung round him like
a suit. His cheeks shone sour. His tongue felt fat.
His sleepstuck halfshut eyes. He sighed. Were these
the fields of freedom? This the journey? Jeez.
The world so clear? His heart went pitapat.
So bright? So lonely? Yup. He pulled his bike

into his arms. He called the deer. They came.
He told the nodding manuka his name.

Commercial Street. A wobbly whirly-whites
and wafty vision frothed outside the Golden
Bay Motels. He squinkled. Jeez. A bride!
She saw him. Chased him. Screamed. 'Gimme a ride!'
Molecule cranked faster. Shit. A Holden
stationwagon flashed its angry lights
behind him. Shitshitshit! She grabbed him. 'Go!'
She jumped. He pedalled. Off they lumbered. 'Quick!
Down there!' They swerved. The headlights drilled straight on.
They shoed a stop. All dark. All still. 'They're gone.'
She kissed him. 'Ta.' 'No worries.' 'He's a prick.'
She foamed away, as brief as melting snow.

The giggling stars. He peeked. He checked. He tiptoed
out of town. The moon unrolled the road.

Pupu Springs, the sign said. Crank crank crank.
The carpark bare. He shat twice in the shed,
then tiptoed through the bushes. Water slid
all round him, silent, massive, swift, like liquid
motorways. He reached the spring. A sign said,
wahi tapu. In he slipped. He sank.
He struggled, water-knotted. Blub. He saw
bright sandflies, moons and greenweeds. Silver sand
danced and glittered on the bottom. Something
held him, bore him, washed him in the swing
of pureclear water, freshed him, grabbed his hand
and pulled him out, and dumped him on the shore.

Flop. He gurgled. Gasped. And giggled. Soon
he fell asleep, dried softly by the moon.

Nana clambered in. The turquoise thronging
bubbles hurried round her fallen skin,
popping talk. She chatted back. The sun
slipped in and blazed her body. It had done
its bit. Been beautiful and babied. Satin
Diamonds kissed her creases. Life and longing
nearly done with. Ah, at last. She smiled.
Her son stood in the shower and soaped his dick.
His body's million daily offers pricked
his tired existence. BumWash lather slicked
mossgreenly down his legs. A golden lick
of sunshine braved his chest. He had a child:

what next? A million more? The gym? No no.
He had a nuddy smoke. The days so slow.

The tracks all traffic-jammed. The carpark full.
The viewer packed. The waters tanking round.
The squealers, moaners, darers, twitchers, campers,
preachers, snackers, skippers, trudgers, trampers,
paddlers, posers – 'Look wha Smelly found!'
Russell Currie capered. Molecule
snoozed softly on the grass. 'A dedman. Phat.'
And soon a crowd. Who soon lost interest. Smelly
slurped one sleeping ear. The Dancing Sands
sparkled in the water. Licked his hands.
The Curries watched, all spellbound. Scratched its belly
round a pedal, waggled, barked – and shat.

'Cool,' said Russell. Water ramped. The crowds
left car by car. And evening pinked the clouds.

75   *Patons Rock like*

He drank of perfect water, picked the bins
and left. He hid from headlights in the trees.
He took a smaller road. Men die alone –
if they're lucky. Easeful and unknown.
Sprayspit, scattered by the midnight breeze,
pattered past his ears. Tucked-up chickens
blobbed the lawns like angels. Stars like jools.
Moonlight like spilt butter. Wind like breath.
Ah, the silly salve of similes!
Their yoking comfort. Us to It. And These
to Those. As if it might be. Life and Death.
He crossed the beach. To this great stage of fools.

Neat housewindows faced the shuttling sea,
to watch for Beauty in Necessity.

And watching thus, but seeing none, he dropped
asleep. The chooks bum-fluffled as the sun
reheated heaven and earth. And stickled round
his matchstick legs. He twitched. The planets wound
their weary way through pointless light. And someone
swam. And someone fished. And someone hopped
along the sand. Driftwood. Tussock. Blue sky.
Red roofs. Clouds and tides. The sun withdrew.
He sat up. Sniff. A barbecue! And beer!
His tummy keened. He dribbled. He could hear
a swish of sizzly laughs. He scrambled through
the grass. Where were they? Came the splash reply –

out swimming! Good! He stormed the grill. He fed
his shirt with stubbies, burning meat and – fled!

He never rode that night. Fatwaves of steak
and fizz broke sour-repeated on his tongue
and splattered in the grass. The houses slumbered,
blindly drawn. Chooks snored. The ocean lumbered
up and down its bath. He hicced. He slung
another splash across the lawn-weeds. Headache,
gutrot, mouthpong, sickwet, fatburns on his
pigeon chest: and shortly-sadly glad
that Evolution mended Man. Whazzat?
A Holden nosed the carpark. Shitshit. Splat!
All down his shirt. Car doors. The urgent pad
of seeking feet. He scooted. 'There he iz!'

He cranked away. Brm-Brm. They're coming. Whoosh!
The bike took off. He shot into the bush.

78   *death of a bike*

He listened while they broke his bike to bits.
It squealed and howled and chattered. Crouching low
amidst the whispering dark, he watched its dying,
broken, silhouetted limbs all flying
past the moon, then pranging. One fat shadow
mimed a cutty-throat his way. He watched its
slow rhetoric sweep and shivered. 'Keep
your fuckin sticky fuckin beaky out
of other people's business, eh!' They chucked
the tangled chain across the road. 'You're fucked.'
The twinkling stars. They wheelied in a spout
of dust. 'Fuck you,' he whispered. Beep Beep Beep.

He laid the bits he found beneath a tree.
And walked away. The houses watched the sea.

He slept beside the highway. Sunshine gripped
his throat. His white toes twitched. The switchback buzz
of bugs around his stinky trainers airing
on a stone. The gloopy tarmac wearing
yellow. Carstreams fanning through his fuzz.
But not that often. DS Baigent dipped
a Twix-stick in his tea. *1st interview*
w. Amy Steffert (39). Blue notelet,
rubber-band, cassette. The sunshine ate
his desklegs. *Missing Person. Jacob Tait*
(26). Richmond swarmed. Sunlit,
sure, the world did what it had to do.

Till evening. Ratas rustled. Rurus squawked.
And Molecule woke up. Arose. And walked.

click–click *Amy Stiffirt* wobble *fiftin*
Bush Strit Rangiora Jacob Tait
was my fianci what? *fianci* hiss
to Willingtin to si my parints Yiss
erm Sunday yiss the 14th whin wi wait
crick–crackle *wi wir nurly* whizzwhizz *Pictin*
whin wi saw this freaky joker bibble
ridin in the dark no lights wi nurly
hittim Jake sez wishdgoback bink
an NO an hi wint mad like HOOJEW THINK
YOU R like ping *hi always does hi rurly*
lostit turnd the bloody van round wibble

yellin screamin an I'll niver whee
forgit hi said WOT HAVE U DUN TO ME.

81 *a knight without a horse*

He slapped along the highway in the dark.
He saw a cow at Onekaka. Whales
in clouds. The song of manuka. And slap ...
slap ... his rubber feet. The loofy lap
of waves at shingle. Wind like shirring sails.
The tick of scented-rag kanuka-bark.
But, ah, the pedal-heartbeat of his mate
was missing, constantyres, the punctious prattle
of its chain, sweet saddle-hug, and all
the cold-straight angles of its love. A pall
of silver slugged the inlet. Crowds of cattle
mooned madeyed against a spattered gate.

He watched the tired tide at Milnthorpe Quay
aslobber. And the moon tied in a tree.

bing *wi chaist im* bong *but hi was gon*
an Jakes got maddermadder ssss *wi drive*
bip *round an round all nite an* what? *an* what?
yiss Monday morning yiss the 15th splot
j-jump *Ive had inuff Jakes screamin an Ive*
made im stop U FUCKIN scusemi MORON
swish *hi's shoutin* swosh *U ROOND MY LIFE*
an all this crap wi what? *wi both git out*
an Jakes got blip *this Kodi Skinner iss*
a what? *a huntinknife hi slasht his* hiss
his rist an whatweep? *leftone* what? *about*
six inchis an hi klap *hi points this knife*

rite at mi shit an sez I'll niver whee
forgit hi yells I JUSS WAN 2 B FREE.

While day punched night away he took the still
backway to Collingwood. And slept among
the shattered graves of hope. The whistled croak
of takapus. Hot dust. The ghosts of folk
who wallpapered the wilderness upclung
from their antipodean beds, all chill
and cheer, and drifted handinhand around
their fallen names, and smiled to call this Home.
Bracken scribbled. Taras twitched and turned
the blueblue sky. His marble mattress burned.
Flies fusselled. Sunlight dripped like honeycomb.
The shivering settlers grinned into the ground.

He lay upon their Work. His skin went red.
Freedom is the dowry of the Dead.

blahblahdateplacetimewherewhatwhenwho
wi wint to wint to Pictin niver sed
a hic *a thing wi stayd at* sss *The Marlin*
gik *Motel wi* what? ticktack *iss in*
um Divon Strit um 33 two-bed
sob *bed* sob *bedroom unit* what? bing *2*
yiss siprit rooms bong *Jake wint out* what? *drink*
I think I smilld it aftir sob *I cried*
myself to yiss to slip nixt morning coff
wi got thi 09.50 Jake wint off
300 sob *an sivin dollars tried*
to find him niver found him sob *I think*

he uh-uh *jumpt O GOD I don't know why*
his niver comin back JUSS LIT MI DIE!

85   Collingwood-watch

He crouched on Tasman Street. And watched its sweet
and dusky dusk unroll its soft-stream souls
through summer's flat surprise. The cafés clinked.
The Motor Camp y-yawned. Wee yachtlights winked.
And watched. The motels nodded. Stars pinked holes
in heaven. Doors shut bump. The empty street.
The bottled lights and larfs. Then just the sea.
Then nothing else that lived but he awake.
He crouched and watched still still: like something sent
to see if Earth was worth the saving. Moonbent
sandgrass shadows. And the whispered ache
of land unpeopled with eternity.

Gargoyled on the Tavern wall, he eyed
his Own and All. And smiled. Kuakas cried.

'Good Riddance, Mum – or Sad To See It Go?'
Jeff & Jack & Nana snaily-strolled
up Rabbit Island. 'What?' 'This year.' The sun
shone silver on the sandy ripples. One
bobbed limegreen kayak like a peapod. Gold
slip-tiding bubbles. 'Nother year tomorrow
eh?' Nana stopped. 'All Hail!' Jack
looked sideways at her brother. 'Yesmum.' Kings
might well have had a hand in such a day.
It set like melting heroes. Far away
the mighty hillheads promised splendid Somethings
soon. All Hail indeed. They started back.

They had a beer at midnight. Rockets crazed
the blockish Oakwoods oaks. The dead sky blazed.

That night he walked to – well, he just walked on.
A country full of hope and resolution
fast asleep. And miles of thoughtless bush.
Plodplodplodplodplodplod. The ceaseless-swoosh
obedient sea. The deadhead consecution
of the stars. Ah, we are here. Then gone.
Like JumpingJacks. Amidst such beauty. Soon
he reached Opou. A car janged past. And stopped.
Reversed. He froze. 'Hey Sunshine, where you goan?'
Two dark-grinned shadows. 'All a–loney–lone?'
'Fuck off you perves.' Oh–oh. The driver dropped
his smoke-end on the road. 'No shit?' The moon

leaned nearer. 'Happy Fucking NewYear, eh.'
'Who gives a shit.' 'Fuck you.' They screamed away.

88   the motel

He flappled into Pakawau at dawn.
That car was parked beside the shop. He watched
the Shadows lock their motel sidedoor. Packs
and boots. A Day Out. Sambos. Anoraks
and watersqueezies. Good. The sky was blotched
with spongy clouds. They left. The motel lawn
flotillarised with ducks. The ranchers open.
In he slipped. First he had a shower.
With all the little soaps. And then a snooze.
Then Fresh Up, Chocolate Wheatens, Peppy Chews,
a mighty shit, clothes-scrub, a Sweet 'N' Sour
Create-A-Meal, some Toffee Pops, a tin

of Palm Corned Beef With Onion, Cheezy Straws
... and sleep. Rain tippy-tapped the grey glass doors.

89 Molecule escapes just in time

He slept like Mr Sleep from Sleepy Town.
The light walked slow across his rib-prowed chest.
The daisy duvet whispered. Drizzle drifted
in the open ranchers. Evening lifted
through the loosening golden clouds. He dressed
and watched TV. The sun sank syrup down ...
a fiddly key! He fled: a sudden shadow
bibbling through the lawn. They yelled. He stopped.
The cupboards banged. The toilet flushed. The TV
blared. He jumped. The ranchers shut ... The sea
wobbled like a rot-plum jelly topped
with newmoon cream. He paddled in its glow.

The caravans switched out. The motel shone
with desecrated sniff. And he was gone.

Bush Road. He twisty-looked and fished the bright
ten dollars, washed and wavy, from his pocket.
Pines lined up against the seaswim buzzed
electric. Something honked. And starlight fuzzed
his fuzzy head. Gawarn. Just try and spend it.
Mrs Sheppard. Donut hair. And three white
roses. 15 grams of rolley. Two
bloo ducks. Two Coppertops. He hung the note
upon a pinetwig in the dark. It flapped
with purplish promise. Days and cars. He slapped
towards Puponga. Moon and wave-edge wrote
their story on the coast. A black swan flew

like Virtue's negative towards a lake
of mud, and shrieked. He watched the tree-ferns shake.

Nestled on the Point amongst fat sheep
and kanuka, he listened to the roar
of hurtling, sunny seas, the thunderous rip
of cattle cropping grass, the clip clip clip
of cabbagetrees. And slept. The bugle-caw
of madblack swans bombardonned in the steep
green fields. He twitched. The ghosts of moa stepped
with giant care in yellow spray. He gaped
asleep. The staring swans scraped overhead
like nazgûl. Perfect. Tarapunga sped
from wind to lifting wind. Mahoe scraped
the wild-lit sky. He clutched the earth and slept.

And nature's teeming, dancing, biting rout
ate up his Self before the sun went out.

That night, unselfed and clean, he left the road
and pattered through some cabbagetrees that spoke
his language. Or he theirs. Whatever. Soon
he reached a vasty beach. A gibbous moon
poured cream-sheen from its urn-mouth through the smoke
of spray. Of which he was. He danced. He glowed.
He twinkled. Akeake on the starlit
steeps all jittered like ... no, not like rootlegs,
Sinners, pleading Branch-Men, Spirits, Ghosts,
not Ever-Evers, Rustlers, Hardwood, Fenceposts,
Dodonaea – um – Viscosa, tentpegs,
skysticks, use or ornament. Just IT.

He capered on the sand. He was the world.
Like nothing bloody else. The moonspray swirled.

DS Baigent mulled the heavydense.
This freaky joker ridin ... something nagged ...
the dark ... *no lights* ... He wondered. Puzzled. Pondered.
Snap! His Twix. He drifted out. He wandered
in his roses ... hm ... his T-shirt snagged
on lovely thorns. He stopped. It just made sense!
Clipped and tugged by little hooks of thought,
inspired by attar-pinks and chocolate-squirt
his brain went *bing!* That crap-mouthed mad-called child!
Cauliflower ... or Hollyhock ... He smiled –
ah – Molecule! He undisclawed his shirt
and strode inside to update his Report.

It took all day. The facts all fat OK.
But why on earth would people act this way?

94 wall

And Jeff laid brick on brick on brick on brick.
Some wall on Gladstone Road. His smoke-smoke strung
its dull, consoling, wasting saws along
a small blue page. The sun shook like a gong
bashed up by freedom. Stodge-slow mortar hung
like too much fat along the wall, all thick
with parching. Jeez. His bolster weighed a ton.
He dropped the trowel. The hose leaked liquid lead.
The wall had reached his neck. He felt his blood
dragging through his costive flesh like mud
through straws. He dropped a brick. His arms went dead.
'Jeff?' Like boulders. 'You alright?' The sun

clashed. He thudded on his knees. 'Oi mate!
Wozzup!' This work. This wall. This world. This weight.

Up and down, up and down, all night
he walked the beach round Fossil Point like some
key-searching ghost, his little bones enhazed
with glow-warp weaved of sand and spray all smazed
with sways of moonlight. Hither, thither, come
and go, and backwards, forwards, graptolite
and glow-worm, bird and stone. But not alone.
Down the beach a man was fishing, black
against the stars, his rod and line as if
holding sea and land together, tensive,
wired, momentous. Still he scuttled. Back
and forth and back like sand against a bone.

The fisher found no fish, the ghost no key.
The sun came up and danced across the sea.

96   Jeff and Jack look at a holiday brochure

'I reckon' – kiss – 'you need a holiday.'
Jeff lay on the sofa. 'Have a beer.'
They smoked. The world was quiet. Sunday gloom
weighed the sunshine in the living room
and aged the too-long tinsel Christmas. 'Here,'
Jack sat down, 'I got this brosha eh.'
They slid the pages, unbelieving. Skies
so blue that Nature would have died with trying,
beaches made of solid gold. Samoa,
Bali, Bondi, Fiji, Noosa, Goa,
skinny people made of copper lying
under emerald palms, hotels the size

of Richmond, special service ... special price ...
meals like ... deals like ... feels like ... Paradise.

This time still. There seemed no need to move.
He sensed All Nature: but its ceaseless, given
action, its provided, busy, ticking
Life had not evolved to free some Thing,
some Mind, some Soul, to think that in this driven,
locked existence It Itself might prove
more kernel to the nature of its kind,
and, undistracted by the soft machine
of living, find some means to contemplate
escape. In Man it had. His tortured fate,
to know, but never bear it, lies between
the works of his existence, and his mind.

Do we deny our souls and call it Peace:
or tend them till they promise us release?

He slept all day, exhausted by his thoughts
that were not thoughts: a driftlog with a clog
of memories it shared with all the world.
A new dark wind brought clotted clouds that swirled
the sky, and gasping backblown trees, hot fog
like ripping rags, ghost-sand and thunder-rorts,
a wind-scut crab, a blindly baffled bird.
He twitched. He sighed. At 2 o'clock the tourist
bus bomped up. All parkas, happy-hurry
photos, wind-squeals. Lightning! Russell Currie
waddled off and pissed amidst the mist.
He saw a faint foot. Phat. A leg. A blurred ...

body! 'DAD!' 'RUSSELL! RAAAAAAAASILL!! QUIIIICK!!!
WE'RE GOING!!!! NEEEEOOOW!!!!' The bus left. 'That was sick.'

The tree was gone. And flies explored the free
white walls. The sun obliged. The gold-wet desk.
DS Baigent eyed the phone. Yes/No.
Was Follicle the Cause? Upon the glow
of molten wood the phone sat, Buddhaesque
and smiling. Hm. If someone passed the sea
and cut his throat then who could blame the water?
Hm ... and yet ... a Plague-sucked man is kept
in Quarantine for others' sake. And knives
and guns have warning stickers. Can our lives
be free of thought *and* danger? Nope. Except ...
what *was* it? Murder? Blackmail? Man–um–slaughter?

Reached ... sat back. Harassment. Politics.
Vick–tim–eye–sayshin. Hm. He ate his Twix.

100   *incitement?*

Witi Jones went back. Beneath Pelorus
Bridge the black, starred water hurled with hush
and mass. The moon rocked on its crescent. Splash!
He plunged amongst the fishies. Tick-tock flash
of trucklights through the bridgestruts. Tickly rush
of gasp and bubbles. And a ruru chorus.
Aaaah. Was this too weird? Who gives a shit.
The bits are here but Mankind Cometh Not.
Which is a waste and why. The less-swift pool
rotated him, dee-lish-ee-uss-lee cool
and nude. The planets swam. And he forgot
that life was Boring, Fat, Inadequate

and Half of What It Could Be. Starlight crowned
the trees. He floated round ... and round ... and round ...

101 Molecule walks to Pillar Point lighthouse and Cape Farewell

He moved. He clambered. Up the steep-short grass.
And up. The sheep sat stolid in the night.
He danced along the Old Man's corpse. The land
made flesh. The winding wind a helping hand.
At Pillar Point he paused. The lighthouse light
a disenchanted beam. Its livid glass
a captive caged. And gorse for guards. He skipped
away. The cliff-gaps yawned. His stomach creaked
like shippy timbers. Water ate its walls.
Too nibbling-slow to see. Just little falls
of dust into the sea. And taras streaked
above, all black on black, like shadows ripped

from one great shadow. Slot-faults. Lime-mud-stone.
And battered bluffs. He danced on. Blown-alone.

Jeff thumbed through the neat wee fales stuck
in golden beaches. Feely palmtrees. Jam
sea-sunsets. Tents at Tadmor. Mum, Molloy
and Me. The caravan at Kaiapoi.
Larking in Tutaki snow. Oh damn.
Oh shit. Oh bugger. Bastard. Bollocks. Fuck.
Birdies pecked the deck. He texted Jack.
wot knd ov fthr lets hz son – oh crap.
Delete. *iv had enuf.* The birdies stopped.
And stared at him with thrill-black eyes. And hopped
away. Delete. *im goan 2 fnd hm.* Tap.
Tap-tap. And flew away. *I wnt hm bak.*

The brochure flipped its pages. Send. Beepbeep.
He had a smoke and cried himself to sleep.

Finished Poet (5). The afternoon,
hung between two Milos and a scone,
rolled its slow warm wheels between the villas.
Nana drowsied. Little living-fillers –
crumbs, the *Mail*, a soup–mug – bibbled on
her outside table. Washing waved. A teaspoon
pulled her happy face into its bowl.
And held her snooze. *Around a swelling bunch*
(5 letters). Giant medicine-bally lemons
dragged their weakling pot-tree down. Their skins
like day–glo. Lumped. Malign. The smells of lunch
and obsolescence blew through Nana's soul.

Sheep browsed through the fence. A twigstalk snapped.
Wham! A lemon fell. The paper flapped.

And down the steep, sheep-shitted, squeezy track
to Wharariki Beach. The rolled back-dunes
held him safely in their quiet vastness.
Their undulating halls. The whispered hiss
of sand attendant round his trainers. Moons
made out of awe and tears hung in the black
and punctured sky. A million stars. Wide-eyed
in slow-mo to the sea. Which like a lumy
skin tried on and on to clothe the sand.
And two great rocks like Warriors of Land
still stabbing up, their army drowned, in spumy
war way out against the doubtless tide.

He stumbled in the shallow-sheets. He ran
the hollow rooms, ashamed to be a man.

The man was dead. His body probly blobs.
His Whys unresurrectable as cake.
But Interesting nonetheless. The Law
Should um Defend the Children of the Poor
And Punish um the Wrong for goodness' sake
which which was what in *this* case? Little throbs
of headache profanised his temples. Light
dab-danced like piss-take fingers up and down
the phonekeys. Right! He rang. It rang. And rang.
And rang. And rang. And rang. A little pang
of heartache pinned his chest. A little frown
of ethics ploughed his brow. It must be Right.

It must be Seen to be. It must be Known
tobedoobedoobe. He parked the phone.

And there upon that random swirl of earth
that men call Heaven, Molecule forgot
the names of things, and then the things, and then
all causes, purposes and feelings men
had conned for consolation ... then the plot.
The world was elements and angles; birth
and death and beauty all unapprehended,
day and night disarmed and thinking still.
The sea not skin, the sand not halls, the rocks
not heroes and the sun and moon not clocks.
As Evolution triumphed, as it will,
awareness of its host existence ended.

Molecule stood up. Then lone and slow
he walked into the Things That Do Not Know.

The silent Buells sparkled through the trees.
Dad's banger gasped behind. The Motorcade
of Sad Salvation. Past the scented hops,
the friendly farmer, sheeps and sheds and shops
and shining sea, the sky like lemonade,
the world like paradise. A blossomed breeze
ballooned behind like benediction. On
and on, sun-flickered, past the deer, the eels,
the perfect waters, bridges, toi-tois, cows
and dust. And all the endless roads that drowse
in sunshine rolled like years beneath their wheels,
tarsealed by Hope and long as Love ... and gone.

Haere ra goodbye. The land, the sea
so gold. A tahou trillies in a tree.